W

The author ha   ⌐xtensively with
Romany families, and has learned many of their
medicinal remedies. Here he lists a number of
common complaints and gives their Romany
cures, provides recipes for some natural wines,
and describes every main ingredient used.

THE ROMANY WAY TO HEALTH

by

CHARLES BOWNESS

NATURE'S WAY

THORSONS PUBLISHERS LIMITED
Wellingborough, Northamptonshire

First published February 1970
Second Impression January 1972
Third Impression 1975

ISBN 0 7225 0152 8

*Made and Printed in Great Britain by
Weatherby Woolnough, Wellingborough
Northants, England, NN8 4BX*

CONTENTS

ABBREVIATIONS USED IN THE RECIPES

tsp.	=	teaspoon	qt.	=	quart(s)
tbs.	=	tablespoon	gal.	=	gallon(s)
pt.	=	pint(s)	lb.	=	pound
oz.	=	ounce			

A WORD ABOUT HEALTH

IN these days of mass conformity many people see the beauty spots of the countryside only from the windows of motor coaches with possibly a description of them given over a microphone by a bored driver or courier.

Quickly the scene has gone, and another takes its place. If the passengers do emerge from their mobile cage it is either for a meal or to shuffle slowly around some building of historic interest.

Perhaps you will congratulate yourself on not being a part of the herd to that extent. You may say that you go off in your own car, where you will, stopping when it suits you.

Yet when you stop, do you get out, or do you sit in the car munching sandwiches and drinking coffee? If you do get out, do you ever go far enough away to lose sight of your precious vehicle?

I am not attempting to denigrate the pleasures of a ride into the country, but rather to pose the question of whether you really enjoy your outings as much as you might.

The apparently easy way out is the curse of modern living; its pathetic result is the regular trail to the doctor's waiting-room, or at least the uneasy feeling of never being quite fit. A nervous state of health can be observed in any public place, from the cafe where women steadily eat their way through sickly-looking confections in between conversations about putting on weight, to the public houses where men can be seen furthering the ruin of their internal organs in a smoke-filled atmosphere.

Today there are only a handful of people left who have managed to escape the excesses and ills of twentieth-century Britain. They are the Romanies, who with sturdy independence have survived centuries of oppression throughout the world since they first came out of ancient India to pursue their endless pilgrimage, never inventing, only perpetuating, living with and utilizing the great inexhaustible powers of Nature.

By Romanies I mean only the true, pure-blooded nomad Gypsies, not to be confused with those pitiful outcasts, the Diddicais, Mumpers, and Posh-Ratts, classed as "Gypsies" only by those unversed in road-lore distinctions.

Among these half-bred wanderers are to be found some wonderful people, but their over-frequent contact with the house-dwelling Gorgio, and the resultant mixture of blood, has produced only too often mobile slums.

It has been my privilege to travel extensively with Romany families, and to have formed lifelong friendships among this most mysterious of all the races on earth. With a typical lack of predictability, they have shared with me the secrets passed down for centuries, have even adopted me as a "brother", and bestowed upon me the title of "Berengro".

Some of this knowledge I am allowed to divulge. May it bring lasting benefit to readers of this book who choose to follow the Romany way to health.

James Crabb, in his book *The Gipsies' Advocate* published in 1831, said: "These inhabitants of the field and forest, the lane and the moor, are not without a knowledge of the medicinal qualities of certain herbs. In all slight disorders they have recourse to these remedies. They are not subject to the numerous disorders and fevers common in large towns".

* * *

A survey by scholars in Germany about 1850 reported that Die Zigeuner or Gypsies of that country were all in remarkably good health. There was not one physically maimed or crippled. Not only did it occur to the Gelehrten that the perfect health and fine physical condition of the Zigeuner was due to their devotion to outdoor life, but that they also had some guarded secret knowledge of herbal medicine which was also responsible for their well-being. Many German peasants today still place much more confidence in the medical knowledge of the Gypsy than in that of "Herr Doktor".

(*Report after Grellmann, 1788.*)

* * *

Even today, in the small towns and villages of Roumania, the medicinal knowledge of Gypsy women is held in far greater esteem than that of the village doctors.

(*Author*)

* * *

According to Frank Cuttriss in his *Romany Life* the Gypsy "lives a healthy, open-air life, with sun, wind and rain as his closest companions, taking no anxious thought for the morrow, with the result that he is seldom seriously unwell or unfit". (*Romany Life*, published 1915.)

Story of the Romany

THEY arrived in England before the end of the twelfth century, those strange, despised outcasts whom we call Gypsies. Even the name is a false one, being a corruption of Egyptian. The wanderers had no real race title. Since, like many Orientals, the Gypsies have a talent for saying that which pleases the listener, rather than that which is true, it was a long time before anyone realised that they originated elsewhere than the regions of the Nile.

In England an Act of repression was passed in 1530: the first of many such measures. The Act forbade the entry of Gypsies into the realm.

There followed four hundred years of varying fortunes for the English Gypsies. Just to be a Gypsy was a hanging matter. Thirteen were hanged in Suffolk alone during Cromwell's uneasy dictatorship. Deportation became common. Gypsies were sent to penal servitude in Jamaica, Barbados, Virginia and, later, to Australia.

In Germany, although Gypsies were hunted down like animals, as a change from wild game, one man showed an interest in them as human beings. He was a philologist called Grellmann who collected words used by them whenever he could overhear them speaking in their own tongue rather than that of their country of adoption. He found that most of their language, as well as its grammatical construction, was identical with that spoken in the Surat district of North-West India.

True, the Gypsies, never averse to casual borrowing, had incorporated words from other tongues into their language. Yet even today words of Sanskrit root far outnumber other words, and the unanimous conclusion remains that the Gypsies spread from India long ago.

The origin of gypsy migration is one of the great mysteries of history. It is very strange that a race of people should have infiltrated from one continent to another for almost four hundred years before anyone became actively interested in where they had come from. And there must have been a time when the Gypsies themselves knew specifically where they had their origins. What dark past could they have been so cautiously hiding?

Few people have suffered for so long, under harsher laws, down the centuries, yet the Gypsies have survived with spirits unbroken. Still the happiest, most light-hearted people in the world, they have danced and sung and played in all circumstances. To the soberest communities they have brought their magic heritage of gaiety, colour and rhythm. Freedom is their life, and life their freedom.

Those who wish to snatch an hour's respite from the pathetic trap of civilization in which we live have created a pitiful imitation of gypsy life. Travel, caravan holidays, even picnics by the car, all a dim resurgence of the instinct which the Gypsies have never lost.

Yet in England today, the Gypsy is regarded as a social problem. The persecution of the dark race is now less physical in intent, though often uncomfortable in a way few house-dwellers can appreciate. It is no joke to be curtly "moved on" at midnight, when the children are asleep. Small wonder that a loose, illiterate community with only a persistent word-of-mouth history should regard its neighbours with some distrust. Gypsy women are the main custodians of the folk-lore of the race, which they memorise as children and eventually pass on, often with embellishments for the sake of dramatic effect.

Gypsies have a magnificent disregard for time sequences, which is difficult to conceive for those who keep diaries, are surrounded by clocks, and to whom the factory siren or the timetable have the urgency of an imperative summons.

What has happened to the Gypsies today? The horse fairs have all but died out, crafts and occupations such as basket making, wood carving, china mending and umbrella faking have no place in a world of mass production. In spite of a faculty for survival, activities become more curtailed and wandering more restricted with every passing year.

Some harassed local authorities, tired of repeated complaints about unsightliness and various depredations are compelling "Gypsies" to move into allotted council houses. But within a matter of weeks these houses are reduced to squalid slums, and complaints are rolling in again.

The mistake made by these authorities is that which authorities usually make wherever they are concerning themselves with the "Gypsy problem". Genuine Gypsies take to the road, leaving the rest to their council houses. The new council tenants are often previously evicted slum-dwellers and miscellaneous erstwhile travellers, but certainly not Gypsies. The do-gooders, with their slightly sinister hopes of mass conformity, have made the common error of assuming that anyone who lives in a ramshackle bus or railway coach is thereby a Gypsy.

Now that the problem is attracting parliamentary attention, here is the solution proposed by the Gypsies themselves. Those among the van dwellers to whom the life is not essentially natural should be re-housed. The question of discrimination thus raised can easily be solved by the Gypsies, for they are familiar with the distinctions of the road-traveller.

For the Gypsies, they should then be allowed the official use of intelligently determined sites throughout the country, and pay for the privilege of camping on them. It must be emphasized that the Gypsies should be permitted to travel from site to site. They must not be compelled to remain in one place, as this would only result in the creation of fresh problems.

With monotonous regularity down the years, from the Arab rulers of the sixth century to Hitler in our own, the epitaph of the Romany race has been written. But the Gypsy is still here, though you see him infrequently. And his own legend says that when the Gypsies find their way back to India they will be travelling amidst the ruins of the world.

A nomad cannot accumulate a weight of property and remain a nomad. Possession spells loss of freedom. Gypsies live for the day and take freedom for granted until it is threatened. Their strength lies in their conviction that freedom of movement is life.

It may be that the Gypsies are right, and that the Gorgio has lost more than he can ever gain.

You may say that you live in houses, warm in winter and cool in summer. That if you are ill a doctor will cure you.

He will reply that he lives in wagons and tents winter and summer. That he does not know the diseases you know, and does not need a doctor until he is compelled to live in a house.

Thousands of years of living in surroundings which contradict their own manner of life has influenced the Romanies but little. Certainly they have adapted themselves to surroundings. Yet the changes they have made have been according to their own processes, and have been from within.

With the spread of the much-vaunted modern progress, a word which really means movement, but which is constantly equated with improvement, much of the herbal knowledge of the past is scoffed at by some scientists. They conveniently ignore the fact that most of their own concoctions are derived from the same plants and are no more efficient.

Herbalists never cure one disease by creating another, as science frequently does. The action of herbs is slow and gentle. Too slow perhaps at times for those immersed in the tide-race of over civilization. Most herbal remedies are pleasant in taste, in contradiction to the idea that medicine must be nasty.

The ancient Chinese had a saying to the effect that the degeneracy of a nation always began when that nation allowed its bread to be made outside the home, inferring that when such an important matter was left to commercial profit, the article was bound to become inferior.

The same might be said of much of our foodstuff and drink, and perhaps also of many of our habits and customs, so greatly are we under the sway of the mass vulgarity of the twentieth century.

To regard the earth and its fruits as something to be beaten back and destroyed is alien to the heritage of man. Let us hope that urbanization and unnatural living is not to be the legacy we bequeath to future generations. The countryside is not just somewhere to motor through at weekends, it is the source of all life.

Let us respect Nature, with the wisdom of the past and the hope of the future.

Romany Medicine

ALWAYS refer to the general information section at the end of the book so that you are sure about the ingredients named.

APPENDICITIS: This is known to the Gypsies as inflammation of the bowels, and I once saw an acute case treated in the following manner by Mireli Gray on a Kentish camping site:

The patient was a boy of about eight years of age. All night long he had been groaning with pain until at dawn his distraught parents hammered on the door of "Aunt Mireli's" wagon.

Knowing of my interest in her treatments, the old Romany "Chi" called me to assist her. When we arrived, the boy had been sick and was lying in the bottom bunk of his parents' wagon. His pulse was rapid, and I guessed his temperature to be over a hundred. He complained of tenderness to the right of, and below the navel. Aunt Mireli instructed the boy's father to get a fire going in the wagon stove.

Then when the oven was hot she took from it a calico bag filled with rock salt and placed it over the affected part.

She continued this treatment, frequently changing the bags of hot salt. Leaving me to heat more bags and keep on replacing them, she then made up an infusion of elder flower water.

This she made in the same way as one would make tea, using 1 oz. elder flowers in a pint of hot water. Then she added $\frac{1}{4}$ oz. oil of peppermint, stirred it well into the mixture, and gave the boy frequent doses in a small wineglass.

After a good rest the lad was as fit as ever he had been. Mireli Gray assured me that she had used this method successfully many times, and that it was a treatment of particular use in remote encampments when it would not be possible to reach a doctor, even if medical aid of the professional kind was desired.

Having seen the treatment successfully used, I have no reason to doubt her.

ASTHMA: The possible causes of asthma are many, and some cases are due to what are now called allergies. A sufferer may unknowingly be affected by emanations from the fur of cats or dogs, or may be sensitive to certain proteins in foods, such as the white of eggs.

Other people have a neurotic tendency to the complaint, mental tensions through overwork causing an attack of frightening shortness of breath.

If the cause is not discovered and dealt with, the unfortunate victim may in time develop emphysema of the lungs and in its train chronic bronchitis.

The foregoing refers to bronchial asthma, which is the commonest type. There are other kinds such as cardiac asthma due to heart disease, and renal asthma due to kidney disease, but it is the bronchial asthma I am dealing with here.

Again it was old Mireli Gray who was the "Mullah-mush-engro", or doctor. The patient was Piramus Vincent, a young man of twenty-seven, and the only

18

true Romany I ever knew to get asthma. As he was an expert horse coper, even among experts, and spent most of his time with the animals, I suspected horse dandruff as the cause of his trouble. He woke up one morning to find it very hard to breathe. While he struggled into his clothes the difficulty increased. Much alarmed, his wife Lendi rushed across to fetch Mireli Gray. When we arrived, it was to find poor Piramus sitting on the seat-locker of his travelling home, arms rigid in front of him and his hands clenched around the brass rail of the little chest of drawers opposite. His head was thrown back, his face pale and covered in sweat, while his breathing was laboured and wheezing.

First of all Mireli told Lendi to make a cup of strong coffee. Piramus managed to drink it and found it beneficial.

His breathing gradually became easier and he began to cough. Aunt Mireli then sent me to her wagon to fetch some leaves. These were leaves from the sweet chestnut tree, and she boiled 1 oz. of them in $1\frac{1}{2}$ pts. of water for 10 minutes. Next she strained off the water and when it had cooled a little she added $\frac{1}{2}$ oz. honey and $\frac{1}{2}$ oz. glycerine.

She gave Piramus a small wine glass full and told him to take the same dose first thing on rising and again after his last meal of the day.

Two weeks later he was completely cured and he has never been troubled with asthma since.

An infusion made from thyme, either fresh or dried, is excellent for asthma sufferers, or for any complaint involving difficulty in breathing, such as whooping cough, or chest troubles.

BLADDER TROUBLE: For bladder disorders boil 1 oz. parsley piert for 1 minute in 1 pt. water.

Strain and take a wineglassful twice a day.

Another remedy is to boil 1 oz. couch grass root in 1½ pt. water for 5 minutes. Strain off the liquid and take a wineglassful six times a day.

BLOOD PRESSURE: To maintain the circulation of the blood to all parts of the body it is necessary that the pressure in the arteries should be kept at a high enough level. The amount of blood in vessels affects the pressure, but the main factors governing it are the action of the heart and the amount of resistance given by the smaller arteries, which contract or dilate as the pressure needs to be raised or lowered.

Blood pressure rises as people grow older, according to their past or present habits in life. If the pressure is too high giddiness and other symptoms arise, and the dangers are apoplexy or cerebral haemorrhage, or thrombosis or stroke. The terms for serious disorder caused by embolism are numerous enough, but it is difficult to make many people realise that they increase the risk of a heart attack by over-eating and by over-indulgence generally.

More exercise, sensible diet, less alcohol—the warnings are familiar to us all.

To assist in correcting your blood pressure boil 1 oz. chopped-up stinging nettle in 1 pt. water for 5 minutes.

Strain off the liquid and boil it again before bottling. Take a small wineglassful three times a day.

BLOOD PURIFICATION: 1: To cleanse the blood there is nothing better than dandelion leaves, Choose fresh young leaves, wash them well and eat them as you like, in sandwiches or chopped in a salad.

2: Nasturtium leaves are also very good for the blood. A mixture of nasturtium and dandelion leaves make an interesting addition to the usual ordinary salad.

3: Another excellent health giver is the common

cabbage. The fresh leaves are good or you can get the juice by boiling a cabbage in very little water. The drained-off water can then be mixed with honey in the same way as the cure given under the heading **Hoarseness**.

4: Raw tomatoes without any additions are also blood-purifiers, but should not be eaten by anyone with a tendency to gout.

5: Turnip tops are yet another wholesome purifier, especially in the spring time.

6: An old remedy for impurities in the blood is to boil 1 oz. burdock root in 1 pt. water for 5 minutes. Strain off and take a tablespoonful of the liquid twice a day. It may be taken more frequently if the case is severe.

7: For people who cannot get much exercise, a tea made from a sprig of groundsel is first class. The infusion should be made in the same way as that given for camomile flowers under **Indigestion**. Cage birds are very fond of groundsel because they do not get enough exercise, and they instinctively recognize the properties in the herb.

8: This excellent remedy for the blood is both a laxative and a tonic. It will clear up eczema.

Take 1 oz. of each of these ingredients: yellow dock, burdock root, and sarsaparilla. Boil them together in 3 qts. of water for 20 minutes. Strain off and add ¼ lb. sugar.

Take a wineglassful three or four times a day.

BOILS: Boils are a result of internal diseased matter seeking an outlet through the skin. If the power of resistance of an area of skin is weakened a boil may appear. Chronic diseases such as diabetes and Bright's disease often result in a general weakening of the skin and this sometimes happens, too, during recuperation from various fevers. All these conditions can produce boils.

In a healthy person, however, a boil commonly appears when an area of skin has been irritated by friction, such as by the wearing of a tight collar. A boil and its surrounding area must be kept clean.

Take some leaves of the herb cuckoo-pint, bruise them and apply regularly to the boil until it is healed.

The pain from a boil can be relieved by dipping alder leaves in hot water and applying to the site of the eruption.

BURNS: 1 lb. primrose leaves put in a pan with half that quantity of the flowers, both simmered with pig's lard, will produce a most useful ointment for the treatment of burns. Strain off the leaves and the flowers and allow the lard to cool for use. This ointment is also good for ulcers and festering cuts.

Another and equally good treatment for burns is an application of equal parts of linseed oil and lime-water.

CATARRH: A severe cold in the head could be described as acute nasal catarrh. It is the inflammation of the mucous surface of the lining of the nose, producing the discharge with which we are all familiar, the "running nose'. When there is little or no discharge, as when a cold is clearing up, catarrh can still be present in a dry form.

On one occasion we were camping by the side of a country lane, intending to move on early the next morning. However, a police patrol car pulled up at about 1 a.m. and we were ordered to leave at once. This entailed rising from warm beds, catching and harnessing the horses, and driving through the rest of the night.

The result for the three families with whom I was

travelling was much annoyance, loss of sleep, and fractiousness from the disturbed children.

On top of this, for me, was a severe cold, with catarrh.

Aunt Mireli came to my aid with horse chestnut tree leaves, thoroughly dried and then steeped in a solution of 1 oz. saltpetre to $\frac{1}{4}$ pt. warm water. The leaves were dried again, rubbed into a powder and I had to burn them on a tin plate and inhale the fumes.

This I did for the two nights after we were moved on and each morning, following Mireli's instructions, I would sniff up my nose a little of a solution of rock salt in water at 1 oz. to 1 pt. water.

The treatment effected a very quick cure.

CHILBLAINS: A chilblain is a local inflammation of the skin and the tissues immediately under it. As those who are prone to chilblains know, they occur on the toes, the fingers, the ears, and the nose.

Caused by cold, the first symptom is an itching, burning sensation. Then the affected part swells and becomes red and the skin is stretched and shiny.

I have rarely seen a Romany troubled by this complaint, chiefly because they are used to an active outdoor life in all weathers. Another reason, I think, is that I have yet to see a hot water bottle in a gypsy wagon.

This cure was passed on to me by Mireli Gray after she had been out "calling" one afternoon. She told me that one young woman had brought from her some cleverly-made artificial roses, which Mireli had painstakingly carved out of turnips dyed with cochineal.

The woman had kindly invited the old Romany chi in for a cup of tea, it being a frosty day. Mireli

23

had noticed chilblains on her fingers, and the woman told her that she suffered from them during every cold spell.

Mireli gave her the following cure:—

1: 2 pt. of water in which parsnips have been boiled without salt. Mix into the liquid 1 tbs. powdered alum. Stir it well, then bathe the affected part in the solution for a good 20 minutes. Let the solution dry without rinsing it off. Keep the rest of the solution for further use until the chilblains are quite gone.

We later learned that the young woman had been successful in getting rid of her complaints, so when she bought the artificial flowers she had really got her money's worth.

2: A good remedy for unbroken chilblains is to dip a raw peeled onion in salt and then rub it on the swelling.

3: For broken chilblains wash a turnip but do not peel it. Put it into the oven and bake it until soft. Then cut it in half and lay a piece on the chilblain, as hot as you can bear it. Afterwards dress the chilblain with a soft rag with Vaseline on it.

COLDS: 1: The perspiration necessary to drive out a cold can be induced in the following way:

Cut up a lemon and place the pieces in a basin. Boil 1 pt. milk and pour it over the lemon. The milk will curdle; it should then be strained off and the curds thrown away. Put the clear liquid into a saucepan and heat it, adding honey to taste. The resulting mixture should be drunk as hot as possible on going to bed.

2: Another cold recipe is to put 1 tbs. black currant jam into a jug with a slice or two of lemon. Add 1 pt. boiling water and stir well. Leave it to settle. This can be taken hot or cold.

3: The nettle infusion given under **Sore throat or chest** will also cure a cold, as will the camomile tea given for **indigestion.** A good hot brew of mugwort tea will also get rid of a cold.

Any of these preparations should be taken before getting into bed. All of them will act as a preventative as well as a cure.

COLIC: Pain due to irregular and violent contractions of various muscular tissues within the body is described as colic. The commonest form is that arising from irregular contraction of the bowel, and this can be due to various causes, such as indigestible food, chill, or constipation.

It is sometimes difficult to distinguish between pain caused by inflammation such as appendicitis, and that due to mere colic; so that unless the colic is clearly due to indigestible food and responds to the following simple remedies, it is well to call in a doctor.

Boiled pumpkin pips well pounded will give a good medicine for colic. Strain off the water.

An infusion of elder flowers or leaves is also a certain remedy for colic.

CONSTIPATION: I make no apology for including this very common complaint, as if it is not properly treated it can become the forerunner of more serious complaints and troubles such as piles, congestion of the womb, colic and indigestion. The absorption of poisons produced by constipation also causes considerable physical and mental depression.

Frequently the causes of constipation are an over-refined diet and lack of exercise. It follows therefore that a rational approach to one's diet is necessary, and at least some coarse, natural food should be included. Wholemeal bread is always better than white bread because it contains bran.

25

Other desirable foods are fruit in general, but in particular raw apples, figs, and prunes; and vegetables, especially cabbage, tomatoes, and any containing a large residue. Honey, marmalade, treacle and porridge are all good. Spinach boiled to a pulp in its own moisture is a good, easily digested laxative, especially for elderly people, but only fresh spinach should be used. It can be mixed in almost any diet.

Some people when affected give themselves a powerful purge, usually one of a number of advertised patents. This is wrong, for this method is followed by an intense reaction on the bowels, causing further constipation, and a vicious circle is set up.

The remedies given here were given to me by Mireli Gray, and by Sylvanus Boswell, one of the "Derbyshire Boswells", a family famous for their knowledge of herbal medicines:

1: Boil together in 1 pt. water 1 oz. jalap root and a piece of aloes no bigger than a pea. After 10 minutes of boiling, strain off the water but be sure to mash up the root to get all the moisture out of it. Drink a wineglassful of the liquid, morning and night.

2: This remedy is particularly good for children as they enjoy it as a food rather than as a medicine. The ingredients are ½ lb. stoned raisins, ½ lb. figs cut up into small pieces, ½ lb. brown sugar, and 1 oz. senna leaves.

Put these into a pan, add ½ pt. water, and stir thoroughly. Then stand the pan in a larger one with cold water in it and boil for 2 or 3 hours. See that the small pan is closely covered.

When you have finished boiling, pour out on to a buttered plate and flatten the mixture to form a thick cake. Leave to cool, then cut into pieces about 1 in. square, and store in a closed tin for use as needed.

One square of the cake is the usual dose, but two

or three may be taken at once without them doing any harm.

3: Put 3 handfuls of blackthorn blossoms into a jar, cover them with cold water and stand the jar in a pan of boiling water for 2 hours. Strain the liquid off and drink a teacupful each morning for at least three mornings. Wait for three or four days and repeat the treatment if necessary.

This is a safe and painless laxative quite suitable for children.

4: This useful remedy is made by taking a dozen senna pods and putting them into a saucepan with a peppercorn, a piece of mace, a piece of whole ginger, about a quarter of a nutmeg, and a clove. Add 1 qt. boiling water, then simmer slowly till the water is reduced to 1 pt. Strain off the water and add honey to taste. Bottle the mixture and take a wineglassful as required.

COOLING THE SYSTEM: 1: In hot weather a healthful and cooling drink can be made by infusing a few flowers of the meadow sweet. Allow it to get cold before drinking it.

2: Another good drink when perspiring, or during hot weather, is a tea made of oatmeal. Boil 2 tbs. coarse oatmeal in 1 qt. water for 1 hour, adding more water as the first boils away. Strain and pour into a jug in which is the juice from 2 lemons and the grated rind of 1 lemon. Add sugar or honey to taste and allow to cool before drinking.

Oatmeal and barley water used to be well-known drinks for men doing hard physical work, such as farm labourers and firemen in the stokeholds of coal-burning ships.

CORNS: As everyone knows, corns are produced on the feet by pressure from tight shoes or boots.

So if this cause is removed, so will be the painful effect.

1: Kenza Boswell once told me a rather interesting way to get rid of corns. The method was to obtain a pearl button and put it in an egg cup and cover it with lemon juice. In about three days the acid had dissolved the button if the egg cup had been covered, and what remained was a thick creamy mixture. This was painted on the corn or corns. When dried it formed a protection from the pressure and could be left on for a couple of days. Then the foot was soaked in hot water, and the covering would come away, bringing the corn with it.

The only objection to this cure is that it becomes increasingly difficult to get mother-of-pearl buttons. As you may have neither the time nor the patience to chip out the inner lining of an oyster shell, here is another remedy for corns:

2: Gather some young ivy leaves, place them in a small jar and cover them with vinegar. Leave them for at least a day, then fix one of the leaves over the corn. Repeat this each day, using a fresh leaf each time. The relief of pain is truly marvellous, and is almost instantaneous.

You may have to continue this treatment for from two weeks to a month, but even the hardest corn will come completely away in time, and you will have no pain at all during the treatment.

Since prevention is always preferable to cure, here is a method of prevention given to me by my dear friend Nat Lee, who never had foot trouble of any kind, and although he was unsure of his age, he was at least eighty when he died:—

4 oz. tallow, 1 oz. powdered sulphur, 1 fl. oz. olive oil. Melt them all together, and stir well while cooling.

Rub a little on the feet in the mornings or before a long walk. No corns will ever appear.

COUGHS: 1: Agrimony, 1 oz. per 1 pt. boiling water as described in the remedy for Diarrhoea, is a very good cough cure and will reduce a high temperature quickly if taken by the tablespoonful three or four times a day.

2: Tea made from the leaves of the coltsfoot is also beneficial for a cough.

3: Also an infusion of the leaves of the eyebright will relieve a cough.

4. A popular Romany cough and bronchial remedy is:
2 oz. coltsfoot leaves, 1 oz. hyssop, 1 oz. of black horehound, 1 oz. lump ginger. Put them all into 2 qt. water and boil down to 1 qt. Strain and press the herbs. When the liquid is cold it can be taken as desired.

5: Another good cough cure is made from:
1 lemon, 2 oz. honey, $\frac{1}{4}$ oz. black liquorice, and $\frac{1}{4}$ pt. white vinegar. Put the vinegar and the chopped-up liquorice into a basin. Place this in a hot oven and stir it until all the liquorice is quite dissolved, or alternatively it can be boiled in a saucepan over a slow heat on the stove.

Add the honey, and when the mixture is cooling add the juice of the lemon.

Take a teaspoonful as necessary.

6: If some ripe black cherries are stewed in very little water, then strained to remove stones and skin they can, with other ingredients, give an excellent relief for coughs. The other ingredients are honey and lemon juice added to the cherry pulp to make it of the consistency of cream.

A teaspoonful should be taken as required.

7: Put a handful of coltsfoot leaves into 1 qt. water and simmer until reduced to 1 pt. Strain off into a jug with a sliced lemon in it. Add honey to taste.

Take a wineglassful three times a day.

CUTS: 1: Minor cuts can be healed quickly by an application of asphodel. A small quantity of this plant is placed in butter and the butter is then melted down to a salve. This should not be used on deep wounds.

2: Take a handful of the herb frogbit, wash it very thoroughly and put it in a jar with ½ lb. clarified lard. Stand the jar in a pan of water and simmer for two hours, stirring often.

The resulting ointment is a fine healer of all cuts and bruises, both major and superficial. It can also be used on spots and broken pimples.

DEPRESSION: 1: Although most of the treatments and herbs described in this book are good for that run-down feeling, a specific tonic is made by taking a handful of wood sage and putting it into a jug and then pouring 1 pt. boiling water over it. Cover the jug with a cloth and leave it for 24 hours. Drink a wineglassful first thing in the morning before eating and another three days later.

The water is not strained off from the jug, and so the infusion becomes steadily stronger.

All Romanies swear by this tonic and Daiena Lee insisted that the three-day interval must be observed for the best effect.

2: 1 oz. hops, dried or fresh, can be infused by adding 1 pt. boiling water. Cover closely and leave it until cold and do not strain it.

A wineglassful three times a day an hour before

meals will provide a wonderful appetizer and general tonic.

DIARRHOEA: The commonest cause of diarrhoea is the presence of some irritating substance in the bowel. In such cases the first thing to do is to get rid of it by making the bowels act more vigorously than ever. If, however, the condition is caused by a disease of the bowel wall, then any purgative would make the condition worse in every way. It is therefore very important to be sure of the cause before attempting treatment.

Ordinary diarrhoea, however, is a symptom rather than a disease, and is usually accompanied by a colicky pain.

For the complaint Mireli Gray had two cures, the first one to be used for what might be called a relaxed bowel condition rather than diarrhoea, and the second one for the more acute kind.

1: Infuse the herb agrimony as if making tea, 1 oz. of the herb to 1 pt. boiling water. A tablespoonful three times a day, usually for two days, will work wonders.

2: Boil 1 oz. rhubarb root for 5 minutes in 1 pt. water. A small dose of this is usually sufficient to cure diarrhoea, but more can be taken, as it is a safe aperient.

The above remedies are for an urgent cure, but another excellent mixture, which is also a wine, can be made from blackberries. This is not only a cure for diarrhoea, but also a preventative for colds and chills, if taken hot. This is the method:

3: ½ gal. blackberries in a preserving pan with 3 tbs. water. Keep stirring it over a low flame until it is a soft pulp.

Squeeze it through a muslin bag. When all the

juice is obtained, put it into the pan again, 1 qt. juice to 1 lb. sugar. Fasten into a piece of muslin 1 tbs. allspice, 1 tbs. cloves, 1 tbs. nutmeg broken up small but not grated, and 1 tbs. cinnamon.

Boil this muslin bag of spices with the juice for 20 minutes, stirring often. Remove the spices and add a wineglassful of brandy or rum.

Bottle the mixture when cool enough, and seal tightly. The dose is half a wine glass for a child, and a full one for an adult.

4: A tea made of strawberry leaves can help in cases of diarrhoea.

DROPSY: This is really a symptom, not a disease. Known medically as oedema, it is an accumulation of a watery fluid in the tissues and cavities of the body. This fluid is always present in tissues and is derived from the blood, but in cases of dropsy the fluid is greatly increased. A common cause is obstruction of the veins, and a tight garter can produce dropsy in a limb. There are more serious causes too, such as cirrhosis of the liver, or a generally feeble circulation can bring it about.

This remedy, as well as being a remedy for dropsy. is also a good kidney tonic: Boil 1 oz. broom in 1 pt. water for 10 minutes. Strain off and take a tablespoonful three times a day.

DYSPEPSIA: This rather alarming sounding word simple means indigestion. It is often caused by over-indulgence in food, or by insufficiently chewing one's food. It can also be caused by too much rich food, and too much condiment, alcohol, or tobacco. If a person does not take enough exercise, this can lead to chronic constipation and, in turn, to dyspepsia.

I have noticed that indigestion usually only occurs

among Romanies when they have been hurriedly moved on and, in consequence, have not had time to properly digest a meal.

It can also occur in young girls with a tendency to anaemia, and Daiena Lee gave the following cure to her daughter Lavaina at a time when the girl was "growing too fast". It was simply an infusion of sage, made like tea, using about 1 oz. sage to 1 pt. boiling water.

This provides excellent enrichment of the blood, and is very good for liver troubles because it cleanses the system.

2: To cure the ordinary cases of indigestion this treatment given to me by my tutor Mireli Gray cannot be bettered: take 1 oz. dried wormwood and pour 1 pt boiling water over it. Let it stand for 6 hours, then strain off into a bottle.

A wineglassful of this twice a day will improve your digestion, and you will be surprised how well and strong you feel in two or three days.

3: Another first-class way to get rid of digestive troubles is to make a hop sherry, which is very simple. Just add ½ oz. of either dried or fresh hops to 1 pt. sherry, and seal the bottle for at least two months. A wine glass of this before a main meal will give you a wonderful tonic.

4: Yet another remedy is to boil 1 oz. quassia chips in 1 qt. water for about 6 minutes. A tablespoonful of the liquor after each meal will soon cure you.

EAR TROUBLES: Many times I have been asked to prescribe for or to treat Ear Troubles. This I flatly refuse to do. *Always* see your doctor if you have such trouble, as it may be a dangerous form of sepsis which can lead to facial paralysis or to a spreading from the antrum into the small spaces of the mastoid cells.

The human ear is a very delicate organ and a blow on it can cause permanent damage and may even affect the brain. For this reason I hate to read of in books or to see in a play, someone having their ears boxed, since it may lead the unthinking to imagine this is a harmless form of punishment.

I know of no Romany who would attempt to treat anything other than a simple earache due to an accumulation of wax. This is done by dropping into the ear a little warm olive oil or almond oil.

On no account must any instrument be inserted, or hairpins or matchsticks or the like be used. This is dangerous.

Anyone suffering from ear trouble should be kept warm until a doctor can see the patient. If a child has introduced a foreign body such as a bead or a pea into his ear, a little oil may be dropped in to ease the pain until the doctor arrives, but nothing else should be done.

Do *not* attempt to syringe out the ear.

I hope the foregoing has been sufficient warning of the dangers of unskilled tampering with the ear.

In the interests of truth I must tell you that there is no herbal remedy or useful home treatment for ear troubles.

EMBROCATION: When an embrocation is needed for anything from sprains to muscular aches, a most effective mixture can be made up in the following way: 2 tbs. olive oil, 1 tsp. Eucalyptus oil, 6 tbs. turpentine, 1 egg, 10 tbs. vinegar.

This is an excellent liniment. The method of preparation is to put the ingredients into a large bottle and shake vigorously before use.

2: Another good liniment is made with ½ pt. household ammonia and ½ pt. turpentine in a quart bottle. Add to this 2 new laid eggs well beaten and with their shells included and finely crushed. Then put in 1 pt. vinegar. Do not cork the bottle at once or it will burst, but leave it until the next day, when it can be corked. The mixture will become creamy and it can then be used on strains, bruises and sprains as needed.

EYES: As everyone knows, the human eye, like the ear, is a very delicate organ, and the eyes should be protected and cared for at all times. Only once have I known a Romany who wore glasses, and it may be no coincidence that he was also one of the few who could read. It is only fair to add, however, that he was aged well over 60 before he required glasses.

1: For inflamed eyes, cold, strong tea is a useful eye-wash, relieving congestion of the lining membrane. This is an astringent recommended not only by the Romanies but also by more than one doctor of my acquaintance. The diluted tannin is the secret.

2: Bluestone is another good eye-wash and strengthener, used as follows. Place enough to cover a 1p coin in an 8-oz. bottle. Fill the bottle with water which has previously been boiled. Shake up the bottle until the bluestone is dissolved. Be sure not to make this too strong a solution, or it will make the eyes smart.

Both the above treatments can be used for inflamed eyes and to wash away grit. An ordinary eye-bath is the best method of application.

For inflamed eyelids and red or sore eyes, here is a good ointment given to me by my dear old friend

Nat Lee, a wise and beloved chief of his clan, and father-in-law of Daiena Lee.

One ounce purified coconut oil, ¾ oz. pure lard, ¼ oz. red mercuric oxide. Warm these ingredients and mix them well. Apply to the eyelids when cool.

As a beauty hint for the ladies mutton fat perhaps does not sound very elegant, but the Romany chis use it lightly on their eyebrows to improve them. Do not use it anywhere else on the face.

To strengthen and relieve tired eyes, two pieces of the peel of an apple bandaged over the eyelids for the night will bring wonderful results. I always use this remedy whenever I experience eyestrain, and the feeling in the morning after this treatment is marvellous. Make sure the apple is fresh and place the inner side of the peel over the eyes.

FLATULENCE: 1: For this irritating complaint, here is the remedy given to me by old Nat Lee, the most knowledgeable Romany of them all.

Take 1 oz. Caraway seeds and bruise them well, then soak them in 1 pt. cold water for 6 or 7 hours. A teaspoonful of this liquid will give relief.

2: For a more serious case which was accompanied by headache, Nat administered clove tea. This was made by putting 3 cloves into a cup and pouring boiling water over them until the cup was half-full. The cup was then covered by the saucer for a few minutes. The mixture should be sipped slowly.

3: The herb fennel is an excellent aid to digestion, and cannot be too highly recommended. First-class chefs use a fennel sauce with salmon for this reason. Wash the herb, and chop it up and sprinkle it over the food. You will find that you will never have stomach upsets.

4: An infusion made from either dried or fresh

mint leaves is also good for flatulence. 1 tsp. in a teacup with a $\frac{1}{4}$ tsp. ground ginger is enough. Nearly fill the cup with boiling water, cover for a few minutes, then add a pinch of bicarbonate of soda, and sip while the mixture is hot.

5: One ounce of spearmint boiled in 1 pt. water for 2 or 3 minutes will relieve flatulence and feelings of sickness. Take a tablespoonful whenever necessary.

FOOT-SORENESS: I have already given cures for chilblains and for corns, but here is a simple remedy for blistered or tired feet which is much in use among Romanies.

Bind alder leaves around the feet under the stockings, and this will ease them miraculously.

If nothing else is available, rubbing the feet with vinegar will harden them and prevent soreness.

I have met Romanies who bathe their feet in goat's milk, and who swear by this as a cure-all for soreness.

GASTRITIS: Gastritis is the medical term for inflammation of the lining of the stomach. The usual causes are either overloading the stomach by eating too much, or the intake of food that is beginning to go bad. The complaint can also be brought about by an excess of alcohol. In short, gastritis is the result of the milder forms of poisoning.

The initial symptoms are dullness, depression and headache. Soon nausea is felt, culminating in vomiting. Frequently the breath is unpleasant and the tongue coated.

Nat Lee, that "gozvero" or wise old Romany swore by the following cure: boil 1 oz. oak bark in 1 qt. water until the water is the colour of whisky. Take a wineglassful after each meal.

GOUT: This painful complaint, once known as podagra, is caused by the accumulation of uric acid in the blood and tissues.

It is not very often found among Romanies because they are well aware of several effective cures for the condition. Daiena Lee gave me this cure:

1: A handful of white horehound leaves, and a handful of black horehound leaves. Boil these together in 1 qt. water, adding more water as the first boils away. Strain the mixture then boil it up again, this time adding a piece of ginger about as big as your thumb. Drink a wineglassful of the liquid three times a day.

2: Another excellent remedy, although it can take several weeks to work, is to slice up a carrot, put the slices in a ½-pt. jar of cold water. Place the jar in a pan of boiling water and let it simmer for 1 hour or more. Strain off the carrot liquid and allow it to cool. Take half the liquid at bedtime and drink the rest in the morning. Repeat this treatment every day until you are cured.

GUMBOILS: Gumboils or other painful swellings in the mouth can be treated in the following way: take 1 dried fig, put it in a saucer and cover it with milk. Place another saucer over the top, and put into the oven. Leave for 20 minutes, by which time the fig should have absorbed the milk and swollen up.

From the middle of the fig cut a slice and place it on the painful area, as hot as can be borne. Repeat the treatment for as long as necessary.

2: Another relief for gumboils and for ulcers in the mouth is to make tea of the dried leaves of the blackberry bush or bramble bush and use it as a mouth wash.

HEADACHE: 1: A few pieces of willow bark boiled in a pan of water is the headache cure of most

Romanies. It is their salicylic acid, the ingredient found in most patent remedies.

2: For nervous headaches the flowery tops of rosemary made into a tea with boiling water are needed. Taken every day, this infusion is good for anyone, but is particularly useful for female complaints.

3: For anyone wanting a supply of nerve tonic, a wine can be made from chopped-up sprigs of rosemary, flowers, leaves and all. Put these into a bottle, about half-filling it. Add ½ pt. sherry, cork well, and leave for a week. The liquid can then be drained off for use as desired.

4: A tea made from a few dried lime flowers will cure a headache in about half an hour. The flowers can be dried on a tin in a cool oven. Leave them to dry for 1 hour or more.

The infusion should be taken hot. It is then best to lie down for half an hour, after which the cure will be complete and lasting.

5: For a severe headache put a pinch of dried marjoram into a teacup. Half fill it with boiling water, cover it with a saucer to allow it to draw, and drink while hot.

HOARSENESS: This is caused by tension in the vocal cords, often resulting in laryngitis. Of the many people I have met in different parts of the world, I know of none with so many cures for this complaint as the Romanies. Since all of the cures are equally effective, the three given here should suffice for any case.

1: This is an excellent remedy, as it is also a cure for other difficulties in breathing and for coughs. Take a good-sized turnip, wash it well but do not peel it. Next cut a piece from the bottom so that it will stand upright. Then cut the turnip downwards into 4 equal slices. Get a deep dish or a soup plate, and fit the turnip together again to stand up in the dish, having first put a layer of demerara sugar or of honey between the slices.

When the turnip has been left standing for a couple of hours, you will find in the bottom of the dish a thick syrup formed from turnip juice and the sugar or honey. This can be taken a spoonful at a time.

2: Boil 1 oz. blackcurrant leaves in 1 pt. water. Strain off and bottle, and take a tablespoonful two or three times a day.

3: Obtain the juice of a cabbage by boiling it in very little water. Mix a little honey with the juice and take as desired. This is also good for asthma sufferers.

INDIGESTION: Although I have already dealt with this under the heading of dyspepsia, I have included it here under the more commonly used name, in case anyone has looked it up for immediate relief.

1: This further remedy is an excellent one, contributed by Esmerelda Price, a Romany woman greatly respected in north Lincolnshire, both in her own community and outside it.

Boil 1 oz. mandrake root in 1 pt. water for 5 minutes. Take a teaspoonful of the liquid five or six times a day. This is also very good for the complexion.

2: As well as being a remedy for indigestion, this is another that will do wonders for the skin and complexion.

If a tea is made by putting a few Camomile flowers into a cup, then infused by boiling water and covered by a saucer for a few minutes, you will find that you

40

have a pleasant drink which will do you a great deal of good. It will very quickly relieve that form of indigestion commonly called "stitch". Drunk regularly, say every morning, Camomile tea will clear up many troubles, especially those caused by liver disorders. Taken hot on going to bed, it will produce perspiration to cure a cold.

3: Apricot marmalade is a pleasant cure for indigestion, as well as being a good natural item for eating at any time. I took this recipe for it from Daiena Lee.

4 lb. ripe apricots put in a preserving pan over a slow fire. Add water to prevent burning. This may not be necessary if the fruit is extremely ripe.

Bring to the boil and simmer for a few minutes. Then strain through a colander, beating well and keeping back the skin and stones. Put the pulp back into the pan with 2½ lb. sugar. Add to this 6 apricot kernels taken from the stones, but blanche them first by putting them into hot water, then remove the skins and cut them into pieces.

Cook the whole mixture slowly, stirring it with a wooden spoon. When it has become a jelly put it into jars for use.

INFLUENZA: In view of the frequency of epidemics of influenza, its debilitating effects, and the possible complications, the disease must be considered a redoubtable one.

1: Whenever an epidemic is raging through the country, it is the practice of my Romany friends to take 15 drops of essence of cinnamon on a lump of sugar, as a good preventative. This appears to be quite effective.

2: Another useful preventative, much used by Kent Romanies, is that of ¼ oz. formalin and 4 oz.

ordinary eau-de-Cologne mixed together in a bottle and well shaken. This is rubbed between the palms of the hands and then breathed in through the nose as an inhalant. Jim Vincent, a likeable and popular member of a well-known Kentish clan, always swore that no germs could exist near this mixture. He used it regularly and was apparently quite impervious to colds and 'flu.

3: Many years ago, when I was travelling in what was then called Palestine, I noticed that workers in orange groves were remarkably free from ailments such as influenza. The orange pickers assured me that the fruit they handled was responsible for this, and that even when the country was swept by the disease they remained immune.

From personal experience I know that eating two or three oranges a day will give one the same immunity.

INSOMNIA: Insomnia can be caused by a number of things and should disappear with the treatment of the symptoms in cases of fever or disease. But for the common, simple kinds due to worry or over-excitement, the following methods are better than any tablets or pills.

1: The pillow stuffed with hops is well known. It is particularly favoured in Kent, and merely working in the hop fields will ensure a good, healthy, refreshing sleep, as I know from experience.

2: If the sleeplessness is complicated by difficulty in breathing, try a pine pillow. Obtain the wood shavings from freshly-cut deal and stuff a pillow slip with them. It is cheap, effective, and quite comfortable to sleep on. The shavings need to be renewed fairly often.

3: Take several flowers of the cowslip and infuse as if making tea. Let it stand for about 5 minutes and drink it just before going to bed. Milk can be added if desired. A tiny pinch of isinglass added to the cowslip tea will rest a weary brain.

4: Some people find that a leaf or two of lettuce eaten shortly before bedtime gives them a sound sleep.

ITCH: Pruritus, to give it its medical term, is due to irritation of the termination of the sensory nerves. The possible causes are very numerous. Certain clothing materials affect some people. Chemical substances in contact with the skin are a common cause of itching in this scientific age. Even excessive use of certain soaps can irritate.

There are also internal diseases and abnormal states of the blood which can give rise to itching such as diabetes, gout, jaundice, and chronic constipation. Drug-taking is another cause.

1: For cases where the itching has proved to be a symptom of eczema, the juice of the bilberry applied directly to the skin is often marvellous in its results.

2: Parasitic complaints such as scabies will respond to the following treatment: 2 oz. lard and 2 oz. mercury mixed very well together until the lard is darkened by the mercury. Wash the affected part of the body with hot water and apply the ointment. The best time for the treatment is just before going to bed.

3: A fine remedy for skin complaints is to cut a slice or two from a raw parsnip and place them in a cup, then pour boiling milk over them. Leave for a little while, and then stir thoroughly. Drink the milk while it is hot.

Even just the laying on the affected part of a slice of parsnip will cure many skin complaints.

43

JAUNDICE: Frequently known as "yellow jaundice" because of its characteristic discoloration of the skin and whites of the eyes. This complaint is not in itself a disease, but merely a symptom of a variety of conditions. All the following treatments are good for jaundice:

1: Dandelion leaves well washed and eaten in sandwiches of thin brown bread and butter are a first-class blood tonic.

2: A tea made from the juice of the herb mousear is another efficient cure for jaundice. In some parts of the country this herb is known as hawkweed.

3: Yet another method for the treatment of jaundice is the use of asparagus in the following way: the root should be washed and sliced, then boiled for 1 hour. The liquid is to be taken by the cupful, three times a day.

4: Nat Lee always tried to include endives or one of the cresses in salads, because he regarded them as an absolute cure for skin troubles. The endive in particular, he maintained, would cure jaundice.

5: For very severe cases, Mireli Gray prescribed 1 oz. barberry bark to be boiled in 1 pt. water for 20 minutes, and the resultant liquor to be taken by the tablespoonful four times a day.

KIDNEY TROUBLES: Here again, these may be due to a number of causes, but in the great majority of cases any of the following remedies will be useful, and in any event will do nothing but good.

1: This remedy, given to me by one of the Lincolnshire Boswells is good for dropsy as well as for kidney complaints: boil 1 oz. of the herb broom for 10 minutes in 1 pt. water. The dose is one tablespoonful three times a day.

2: Boil 1 oz. Cranesbill root in $1\frac{1}{2}$ pt. water for 20 minutes, which should reduce the amount of water to about 1 pint. Take a small wineglassful of the liquid twice a day.

3: 2 oz. burdock root boiled in 4 pt. water until the water is reduced to 1 qt. makes an extremely good remedy for kidney ailments. Drink the liquid as required.

4: A weak infusion of the berries of the barberry is also good for kidney trouble.

5: It is very beneficial to drink the water in which leeks have been boiled. It is also good of course for sufferers from kidney disorders to eat leeks.

LUMBAGO: All Romanies believe that a small raw potato sewn in a little bag and carried about the person is a certain preventative of rheumatic disorders such as lumbago.

It may be that the reader will dismiss this as sheer nonsensical superstition. However, of all the hundreds of "travellers" I have known, I have only ever met one who was afflicted in this way.

Poor Lucy Smith attributed her rheumatism to a curse which she had invoked, and thus gave me the material for a story entitled *How Lucy was Bewitched*, published in a well-known magazine.

But for those who regard themselves as being free from superstition, the following advice is well worth taking:

Celery is the great remedy for lumbago and kindred complaints such as sciatica and rheumatism. Allied to an almost meatless diet it will work wonders. Do not take sugar, and eat as much vegetables and fruit as you can. Fish can be taken, and a little poultry occasionally.

The chief part of the diet is celery, which must be

taken in one form or another every day. If fresh celery is unobtainable, then take celery seed. The seed should be stewed in milk, then strained, and the liquid taken three times a day between meals.

Fresh celery should be boiled in milk and the milk allowed to cool for drinking.

The longer you have had your complaint, the longer will the cure take, but even the most chronic cases will show improvement if you persist with the treatment.

MEASLES: This common fever occurs about every two years as an epidemic. One attack usually gives immunity for life, though contrary to general belief, this is not always so.

The only remedy I have ever heard of among the Romanies is this one which Nat Lee successfully used on his grandson Dinki:

A tea made from saffron will induce the necessary perspiration in the early stages to throw off the fever.

NEURALGIA: This intolerable pain is that which travels along the course of a nerve when no structural changes can be observed, even with a microscope.

1: Mireli Gray had an absolute cure for this condition: a dressing of horseradish scrapings held to the site of the pain will draw it away.

2: Another remedy, supplied by Daiena Lee, is to boil 1 oz. of the herb ladies' slipper root in 1 pt. water for 10 minutes. Strain off the liquid. One wineglassful should be enough to offset the attack.

PILES: This distressing complaint is all too common, but I have yet to meet a Romany who did not believe that a sprig of the herb pilewort carried in the pocket would give a complete cure.

However, for those not possessing such faith, the following method will be found useful:

An infusion of the herb drunk four times a day, about a wineglassful at a time. Like so many other herbs, pilewort should be infused in the same way as tea.

For an external ointment, here is an excellent mixture: 4 oz. pure unsalted lard, 4 or 5 ground ivy leaves, 1 oz. Plantain leaves. Boil all together for 10 minutes, pressing the leaves well into the lard.

Strain off for use when cool.

QUINSY: This old-fashioned name is that given to what is really a suppurative form of tonsillitis. The only Romany cure for this I have been able to find is this one given to me by "Auntie" Queenation, a remarkable old character who knew much but would reveal little:—

Boil the herb cudweed in 1 pt. water for 1 minute. A tablespoonful of the liquid should be taken twice a day.

The liquid can be used as a gargle at any time, and will prevent throat troubles.

RHEUMATISM: Although one cure for rheumatism has been given on the page dealing with lumbago, here is another which I once heard Nat Lee give to a farmer who had kindly allowed us to spend a few nights in one of his fields in Norfolk:

1: Boil 1 oz. dandelion root in $1\frac{1}{2}$ pt. water for 20 minutes, which should reduce the water to about 1 pt. Strain off and cool, and take a wineglassful twice a day.

2: Another remedy, this time one of Mireli Gray's, is to take a handful of hops and pour boiling water over them until they are quite soaked, then place the hops in muslin to keep them together, and lay them on the affected part. This simple poultice is excellent for long-standing pain in stiffened joints.

3: An equally simple treatment for rheumatic pain is one similar to that described for neuralgia, only in this case the horseradish is used without being scraped. Just peel the root of a horseradish, cut it into slices and rub them on the affected parts.

4: Yet another simple application is that of dried marjoram placed in a muslin bag and heated in the oven, then put on the area of pain.

5: An infusion of the leaves or flowers, or of the crushed seeds of burdock will also relieve rheumatism. The first of these methods will cure rheumatism if it is caught in time, but the other external methods are good ways of relieving pains in the joints for chronic cases.

SCIATICA: 1: The herb rue is first class in its properties for relieving sciatic pains. The green leaves of the herb are beaten and bruised, then laid on the site of the pain.

2: Teni Lee, youngest and seventh son of old Nat, gave me this cure for sciatica. Make a tea of the herb ragwort, in proportions of 1 oz. to 1 pt. water. The dose is a wineglassful three times a day.

SORE THROAT OR CHEST: Make an infusion of the herb self-heal as if making tea, one pint of water to 1 oz. of the herb. Drink the liquid very slowly, a wineglassful two or three times a day.

2: The crushed root of the herb avens will provide another cure for a sore throat if a little is placed in boiling water for a few minutes. The liquid is drunk cool.

3: A raspberry vinegar made by putting a quart of fresh raspberries in a basin is good for sore throats and chests. Pour on a pint of vinegar and cover well. Let it stand for 3 days, stirring it each day. Strain through a flannel bag and add to the liquor 1 lb. loaf sugar to each pint. Then boil for 10 minutes, removing the scum which rises to the top. When cold, bottle and cork well. Best taken from a spoon and sipped slowly.

4: If nettle leaves are boiled down, and honey added to the water to make a syrup, a teaspoonful will clear the throat and heal the chest.

5: Take 3 dried figs, split them open, and put them into a saucepan with 2 pt. water and 1 oz. liquorice root. Simmer to about 1 pt., strain off the liquid and bottle it. This will provide you with a most effective gargle for a sore throat.

6: Perhaps the best infusion of all for chest and throat trouble is linseed tea made in the following way: put 2 tbs. of whole linseeds into 1 qt. water and simmer slowly for about 70 minutes. Strain off the liquid and add the juice of two lemons and sugar or honey to sweeten to individual taste.

The Romany women tell me that this drink is also helpful for expectant mothers, and claim that drunk daily during the last few months of pregnancy it will ensure an easy confinement, especially if three raspberry leaves are added to the simmering linseed.

SPLINTERS: An excellent way of drawing out splinters in the flesh is by filling a narrow-necked bottle with hot water and emptying it again when the glass is as hot as possible. The neck of the bottle is then tightly placed over the splinter, and as the bottle cools down a vacuum is created which sucks the splinter to the surface.

Be careful to handle the bottle with a cloth, and not to get it so hot that it cracks or breaks.

SPRAINS: A very strong decoction of camomile flowers, infused by pouring a little boiling water over them and then allowing time for it to draw, will relieve the pain and stiffness caused by a sprain. Apply externally while hot.

STINGS: The juice of the pimpernel is an excellent remedy for bee and wasp stings, and other insect bites.

THRUSH: This ailment is caused by a fungus which grows on a mucous membrane. It is commonest in children, although it can occur in a debilitated person of any age.

The treatment here is one supplied by Daiena Lee, who had used it on her own children, Dinki and Lavaina.

Biborate of soda, commonly known as Borax, should be mixed with honey and applied to the patches. This will clear up the fungus.

TOOTHACHE: 1: I have known many Romanies who relieve an aching tooth by going to the chemist for a small bottle of oil of cloves and then applying a drop of this to the tooth. This is, however, an expensive method, as the oil is dear.

2: A much cheaper means of relief can be found by using the juice of a white beetroot.

3: Sage tea, used hot as a mouth wash may also be effective.

It must be remembered that these methods can only relieve and not cure, and in the final resort one must visit the dentist for a permanent cure of the trouble.

As an occasional teeth whitener, lemon juice is excellent. It should not be used too often however, as it is acid.

Strawberry juice will also whiten teeth.

ULCERS (External): 1: For ulcers on the skin I cannot give a better remedy than this one passed on to me by Nat Lee: chop up some leaves of the herb fluellin and mix them with pure lard, making an excellent ointment.

2: Raspberry leaf tea is a good preparation for cleaning external ulcers and sores.

VARICOSE VEINS: The elderly Romany lady known as Auntie Queenation always amused me by her insistence in calling this complaint "various veins". Whatever her lack of knowledge may have been of English usage, there was little she did not know of natural remedies.

She gave me the following cure, and although I was never able to see it in action, my faith in Auntie Queenation as a wise woman is boundless, for I witnessed several of her other successful cures.

When a vein becomes knotty and dilated, it is said to be varicose. This usually occurs in the lower leg.

Auntie Queenation's cure consisted of applying cider vinegar to the affected veins night and morning. This, she told me, would eventually reduce them if the treatment was carried out faithfully for a few weeks.

The rest of the treatment was to drink apple cider vinegar in water two or three times a day, and to observe a sensible natural diet.

WARTS: 1: Dandelion juice is the surest cure for warts. Squeeze a leaf and a drop of the milky secretion will appear. Apply this to the wart and continue this treatment for as long as is necessary. Eventually the wart will turn black. If you carry on this treatment, you will suddenly realize to your surprise that the wart has gone, leaving no trace.

2: Apple juice can be used as an alternative cure by rubbing the wart with a slice of freshly-cut apple and leaving the juice to dry on.

3: Juice of an elderberry leaf may also be used, or that of chickweed. The greater celandine and the houseleek may also be utilized in the same way, but the best juice of them all is that of the dandelion.

4: One's own morning spittle can be used on warts and it will remove them in time. But the process is a long one and the method must be applied on waking, before food or drink is taken.

A word on prevention of warts. The water in which eggs have been boiled can cause warts. Such water should always be thrown away and not left standing about. Warts can also be picked up if the skin is scratched on the walls of farm buildings such as cattle byres, stables and so forth.

As a final warning, warts should never be cut or pricked, except under medical supervision.

WHOOPING COUGH: 1: Medically known as pertussis, whooping cough can be cured by boiling 1 oz. of the herb mousear, or hawkweed as some call it, in 1 pt. water for 3 or 4 minutes. Strain off the water and drink a wineglassful four times a day with a spoonful of brown sugar added.

This is a wonderful tonic.

2: Almost as good is an infusion of dried thyme.

A pinch of this in a teacup will suffice. Half fill the cup with boiling water, cover with a saucer for a while, then take a few sips each time the cough is troublesome.

3: Yet another remedy is that of the turnip cure given already under the heading of hoarseness.

4: For whooping cough in an adult the following remedy is useful: a horseradish should be scraped until you have half a teacup full. Add vinegar but do not cover the scrapings. Have just enough vinegar to soak the horseradish when it is pressed down. Leave the mixture for 24 hours, pressing the scrapings down from time to time.

After the 24 hours are up add a tablespoonful of glycerine and mix well into the concoction.

Take half a teaspoonful in a wine glass of hot water.

5: Similar to the turnip cure for whooping cough and hoarseness, is a medicine made by scooping out the insides of several large radishes and filling the cavities with black treacle. Leave standing for two days and then take a teaspoonful of the liquor three times a day.

Radish leaves are also good in salads.

WORMS OR FLUKE: All fresh vegetables used in salads, such as watercress should be very thoroughly washed. Wild watercress in particular should be carefully prepared, as the eggs of trematodes, or flukes, can be swallowed on them, resulting in the parasitic complaint known as worms.

1: A brew made from the roots of the male fern, of 1 oz. in $1\frac{1}{2}$ pt. water, boiled up and strained, will give a mixture that will eradicate worms. No food should be taken for a few hours before going to bed, and in the morning a wineglassful of the liquid should be taken.

2: A boiling of elder bark and elder flowers, prepared and taken in the same way as above will also provide a cure.

3: An infusion of the leaves or flowers of the bindweed also expels worms.

4: Nat Lee once told me of a rather unusual way of expelling worms. The method was to pour hot water over peach leaves and then to lay them on the stomach. Nat stated that this simple poultice was remarkably effective.

On no account must any peach leaf preparation be taken internally, for the leaves contain the poison prussic acid.

Grow Your Own Herbs

ONE of the saddest things about modern life is its increasing urbanization. Contemporary economic historians are now of the opinion that the Industrial Revolution cannot really be set within specific dates as it is still going on, feeding as it were, upon its own momentum.

Many people suffer from an unconscious feeling of anxiety or depression, owing to the conflict within between the values of the old order of rural living and the increasing pace of scientific events.

Even townspeople are frequently aware of the lack of natural conditions in their daily lives. Some forty years ago the chief illnesses and complaints were of the digestive system, whereas now they are usually of the nervous system.

Trained herbalists are much less common today, and since large areas of the countryside are subjected to spraying and to so many other direct and indirect forms of pollution it is often very difficult to find required herbs.

When found, it is not always possible to tell whether or not the herbs are safe to use, because of these factors. Therefore the most practical and enjoyable way of providing yourself with useful herbs is to grow them yourself, assuming that you are fortunate enough to possess a garden.

It will not be possible to grow them all, as some of them are imported from very different climates, and some, such as liquorice and horseradish are not practical within the confines of an average garden.

It is a good idea to surround your garden by a hedge which is in itself a good herbal source, and which in any case is far more natural and beautiful than the brick wall, or worse, the wire fence. The choice of hedging is a personal one, but blackthorn is popular and can provide you with sloes as well as flowers. Or you may prefer a bay hedge, an evergreen which will provide aromatic leaves which are useful in cooking.

The value of freshly-gathered produce from your own garden cannot be over-emphasized. So here, in alphabetical order, are some suggestions for your own herb garden, omitting those herbs previously mentioned.

BALM (*Melissa Officinalis*): Can be raised from seeds or cuttings in April or May. It does best in a light soil. The leaves have a lemon fragrance and make refreshing tea. Much honey is contained in the flowers. It is useful in the kitchen for stuffings. A perennial, balm grows to about 2 ft. The finely chopped leaves, fresh or dried, can be used instead of mint for sauce, made in the same way.

BASIL (Sweet) (*Ocymum Basilicum*): Also raised from seed, basil should be planted towards the end of May. It needs a well-drained, sunny bed. The leaves are used for flavouring soups and stews, sausages, and tomato dishes.

BERGAMOT (*Monarda Didyma*): Best obtained as rooted cuttings. Bergamot is a weak plant and must be kept free of weeds. Its perfume is most refreshing, and a tea of its leaves is as good as anything that can be bought.

BORAGE (*Borago Officinalis*): This hardy annual should be sown in April and allowed plenty of space. Sprigs of borage put in fruit drinks or in wine impart a delicious flavour, and makes the drinks cooling. It is a member of the forget-me-not family and grows to about 1 ft. 6 in.

CHIVES (*Allium Schoenoprasum*): Can be raised from seed and later on clumps may be divided to increase the stock. The young shoots can be chopped to make a delicious addition to soups and salads and egg dishes. Chives belong to the onion family. It is best grown in moist ground.

SAVORY (Summer) (*Satureia Hortensis*): This is an annual sown in April. The herb can be used in stuffings, in soups, and also cooked with broad beans.

Winter savory is similar in flavour and can be used for the same purposes.

TARRAGON (*Artemisia Dracunculus*): A perennial growing to about 4 ft., the chief use of tarragon is for making vinegar. It is a good flavouring for pickles and sauces. A few leaves can be added to salads.

I hope that these brief notes will encourage those of my readers with gardens to an interest in the study and practical application of herbal lore.

Now a word about the drying of herbs. Most herbs can be used either fresh or dried. As a rule, herbs to be dried should be gathered on a dry day when plants are well developed, and just before they flower. Rinse the cut plants in cold water, shake them thoroughly and tie them in small bunches. Large bunches tend to go mouldy in the middle. Hang in a dry, airy place. When the bunches are quite dry and crisp, remove the leaves from the stems and rub them through a fine sieve. Store them in airtight jars, as full as possible, in a dark place.

What are known in culinary parlance as "fines herbes" are a mixture of equal quantities of chopped fresh parsley, chervil, chives, and sometimes tarragon. These are sprinkled on omelettes, scrambled eggs, and salads.

"Mixed herbs" usually means sage, parsley, marjoram, and thyme, with other additions if desired. They are used for flavouring meat or fish dishes, or for stuffings.

A "Bouquet garni" comprises two or three stalks of parsley, a sprig of thyme and marjoram, and a bay leaf. These are tied together with thread and added to foods being cooked in stock or water. If dried, the herbs are tied in a muslin bag. They are removed before the food is served.

Some Herb Wines

THE usefulness of herbs is not confined to remedies for illness and to culinary purposes. Many wines can be made from them also, and quite simply.

Here are a few recipes which may stimulate an interest in this fascinating subject of natural living. The beauty of making these natural wines is that there are really no definite rules. Country people and the Romanies have always experimented, being familiar with the ingredients they have used. Before tea-drinking became general, home-made drinks were a necessity to the poor, and even the rich who could afford imported wines by no means despised some of the excellent products of the farm cottagers.

One interesting aspect concerning what have been called "country wines" is that a genuine herbal drink will never give one a hangover. The hangover is something that science gives. I do not make this statement in order to encourage over-indulgence, but to show that home made wine is, properly regarded, a valuable addition to the sadly depleted modern diet, being wholesome, and an innocent art of our forefathers.

It should be remembered, however, that some of the wines are potent, and that there is no excuse for over-indulgence in them any more than over-indulgence in anything else. They should not be given freely to children, or be taken incautiously.

Most of these wines can be made quite cheaply, at a cost of not more than a few shillings a bottle. The equipment needed is an earthenware bowl big enough to hold at least 1½ gal. liquid, such as a bread puncheon with a wide top. Also needed is some muslin for straining, a 1-gal. glass jar, a large wooden spoon, some new corks, a length of rubber tubing for siphoning and, of course, a supply of bottles.

All the equipment must be kept scrupulously clean and it is most important never to ferment wine in anything but glass, wood, or earthenware containers.

Ordinary enamelled kitchen saucepans can be used for boiling.

Wine will not ferment in a cold place. Add the yeast when the liquid is at blood heat, and keep it in a temperature of about 60 degrees F. Always cover fermenting wine to prevent microbes from entering it which may cause it to go vinegary.

When filling your glass jar you can top it with a cork, but better still is to use a special trap. These cost only a few shillings and will allow gas to escape without letting air in.

It is possible to make good wines using baker's yeast—which must be fresh—or you can use dried live yeast. This will keep for months and has about twice the strength of fresh yeast, so if you use this, use only half the given recipe quantity. The best way of using baker's yeast is to spread it on a lightly-toasted slice of thick bread. This should be allowed to float on the surface of the wine. There are special yeast preparations sold for boosting fermentation, but you can use instead the juice and thin rind of two lemons.

It is best for the beginner to stick to stated recipes until such time as he feels experienced enough to make his own experiments.

Nature produces its own fermentations, and treating the ingredients with respect and patience will give you good results in proper proportion.

"Scientific" methods of distilling, chemical fermentation and too-violent clarification really upset the natural balance of ingredients and produce the commercial drinks with a "kick".

Home-made wine is light and pleasant to the palate and without the sharp taste of spirits, and also without the more disagreeable aspects of commercially produced drinks. Home-made drinks are also more satisfying, and therefore less likely to be taken to excess.

From antiquity until the end of the nineteenth century, most of the beer and wines consumed by the people of Europe were made at home. In Britain beer was brewed every quarter by the cottagers, and usually once a month in the rich houses. As the herbs came into season, the different wines were made. Brewing was an art taught to every girl, as much a part of her domestic education as bread-making, cookery, and needlecraft. Many men were also adept. Ale houses and inns kept high standards because the majority of people were natural connoisseurs, knowing as much about brewing as the proprietors. Home-made beers and wines were highly esteemed for their medicinal properties, which were well understood. Drinking to a person's health was a reality, as well as being part of rural hospitality.

The heroic era of the fast clipper ships brought a change in the habits of most people, for tea was made accessible to practically all, since most of these fast ships were engaged in the tea trade.

Where the family of Jane Austen had written letters to each other frequently referring to the state of their wines such as mead, red-currant, and so on, and where George Eliot and Thackeray were able to write into their novels accounts of rural hospitality, there now came a trend towards the new fashion for drinking tea.

The far-sighted railed against it, William Cobbett called it poison, and the Religious Tract Society denounced it. The need for teetotalism came much later with the great spread of commercial breweries. Tea, regarded by its opponents as a menace, won the day, and in direct line of descendancy from the victory of the foreign weed we have snack bars, milk bars, tea parties, public houses, canteens, and licensing statutes of increasing complexity.

And so today the custodians of the real heritage of home-made wines and other drinks are those people in the remoter countryside, who are regarded as old-fashioned or reactionary, and Romanies, who instinctively prefer that which can be naturally produced to that which can be bought.

BALM WINE: Take 2 qt. balm leaves into your earthenware dish. Then boil together 1 gal. water, 2 lb. sugar, the juice and rind of 1 lemon and the well-beaten white of 1 egg. Skim well and strain the liquid on to the balm leaves, stirring well until cool.

Next put in a piece of toast that has been spread with yeast and leave it to work for three days, then strain the liquid through muslin into jar or cask, keeping well filled.

The liquid will then hiss slightly for about an hour. Bung closely when the hissing stops, as this indicates the end of the "working".

The wine will be ready for bottling in three months, and is an excellent remedy for nervous disorders, for this herb is of the same family as the "balm of Gilead" of Biblical fame.

BEETROOT WINE: Boil 4 lb. beetroot in 1 gal. water until it is tender, strain off the liquid and add 4 lb. sugar, stirring until quite dissolved.

When the liquid is cool add 1 lb wheat and 1 oz. yeast on toast to float. Ferment for fourteen days, then strain off and bottle.

The original boiled beetroot can be covered with vinegar and eaten. It need not be thrown out.

CAMOMILE WINE: For this take 1 qt. camomile leaves and ½ pt. wormwood leaves carefully picked from their stalks. Put them into an earthenware dish and bruise them together. Add 1 oz. camomile flowers and 1 oz. of rosemary leaves. Boil 2 gal. water with 6 lb. clear honey in it, and then pour the boiling liquid over the leaves. Cover the dish closely and leave for 4 days.

After that warm the liquid to a good fermenting temperature and stir in 1 oz. of yeast and allow it another 4 days.

Strain off the liquid into a cask and add 1 oz. dissolved isinglass. Quite fill the cask and when the liquid stops hissing, bung it closely.

Keep for nine months before bottling, and seal the corks. Some people add brandy to make a very strong wine, but if this is done the healing properties are lost.

Unadulterated camomile wine is very good for the digestive system as it cleans the stomach and normalizes the temperature. It is slightly bitter, but very strengthening.

COWSLIP WINE: Boil 3 lb. sugar in 1 gal. of water for ½ hour, skimming the water. Grate the rind of 2 oranges and 1 lemon, and put into a big pan with the juice of all three fruits. While the sugar water is boiling pour it into the pan too, stirring well.

When the liquid is cool but not cold add 4 qt. fresh cowslip flowers. Next add 2 tbs. of brewer's yeast. Stir very thoroughly, cover with a cloth, and leave standing for 48 hours.

Put the mixture into the fementing cask, stop it up and leave for two months.

After the two months are up, draw off the liquid, strain it, and bottle. Leave for at least a month before drinking, but the longer it is left, the better it will be.

This is a wine which is a good nerve tonic and gives refreshing sleep. For anyone, including children, suffering from a feverish cold, a glass of it added to hot water and drunk in bed will bring about a cure.

DANDELION WINE: The ingredients for dandelion wine are: 1 gal. dandelion flower petals, 1 orange, 1 lemon, 3 lb. sugar, 1 oz. of well-bruised ginger root, and ½ oz. yeast on toast.

First wash the dandelion petals well and cover them with boiling water. Allow them to stand for 3 days, stirring often and squeezing the flowers.

Strain off and add to the liquid the thin rind of the lemon and orange as well as the fruit sliced up. Boil for ½ hour in 1 gal. water and allow to cool.

Spread the yeast on toast and float it in the liquid. Ferment for 6 days and then put it into your glass jar. It can be bottled after it has cleared.

Dandelion wine is good for the liver and the digestive system generally.

ELDERBERRY WINE: This will give you a wine which tastes like port. Pick 2 qt. elderberries, wash them, and boil in 1 gal. water for 15 minutes.

Strain off the liquid and add 3 lb. sugar and 8 oz. raisins to it. Simmer gently for 20 minutes. Allow the mixture to cool then add 1 oz. yeast on toast. Cover well, leaving to ferment for fourteen days.

Strain and bottle, corking lightly until fermentation stops, then bung tightly and keep for twelve months.

Taken hot with honey, elderberry wine is a good cold cure.

ELDER FLOWER WINE: 1. Take 1 pt. elder flowers and put into 1 gal. water and simmer for 15 minutes. Put into a bowl and add $3\frac{1}{2}$ lb. sugar, 8 oz. raisins, and 3 sliced lemons. Stir the sugar until dissolved and when the water is lukewarm sprinkle $\frac{1}{2}$ oz. yeast on to the liquid. Allow to ferment for fourteen days, then strain carefully into a jar. Do not disturb the sediment at the bottom, leave for a while, and then bottle.

ELDER FLOWER WINE: 2. Another wine can be made from elder flowers in the following way:—

Add $2\frac{1}{2}$ pt. elder flowers to 1 gal. boiling water and boil for 20 minutes. Put in 2 lb. honey and 1 lb. sugar and the rinds and juice of 2 lemons and 2 oranges.

Boil again for another 20 minutes and when cool add $\frac{1}{2}$ oz. yeast. Let the mixture stand for 24 hours and then strain into a cask or jar. Keep for at least six months.

Elder flower wine has the same qualities as the elderberry.

HOREHOUND AND WORMWOOD BEER: Boil together for 2 hours in 10 pt. water 1 oz. horehound, 1 oz. wormwood, 1 oz. hops, 8 oz. malt. Let the water only simmer after it has come to the boil.

After the 2 hours strain off the liquid into an earthenware vessel. Add 2 oz. brown sugar and 1 oz. yeast. Cover for 24 hours.

Skim and bottle the liquid. Put the corks in lightly, and tighten them up some 12 hours later.

The beer will be ready for drinking in a matter of a week but will increase in strength the longer you leave it.

This is a good general tonic.

PARSNIP WINE: Clean 4 lb. parsnips, cut them up and boil in 1 gal. of water until tender, then strain. Add 3½ lb. sugar, 1 oz. of lump ginger, 1 oz. dried hop flowers to the liquid, and boil for 5 minutes.

Put the mixture into the fermenting bowl and add to it the juice and rind of 1 lemon and 8 oz. chopped unstoned raisins. Allow this to cool before putting in 1 oz. yeast on toast and 8 oz. wheat. Ferment for fourteen days, then skim and bottle. Keep for twelve months before drinking.

This is very good for the skin and system generally.

POTATO WINE: Put 1 lb. wheat, 1 lb. raisins, and 1 lb. chopped potatoes into an earthenware bowl, add 4 lb. sugar and cover with 1 gal. warm water. Add 1 oz. yeast and leave to ferment for three weeks. Then strain off and bottle.

This is a good wine for beginners to try as it is simple and relatively quick to make. The result is a fine golden wine.

RAISIN WINE: Choose large, sound raisins— 10 lb. are needed, and 1 lb. sugar. Chop the raisins finely and pour 1 gal. boiling water on them. Strain off the liquid and squeeze the remainder from the fruit. Leave the liquor to stand for twelve hours, then add the sugar and leave it to ferment.

When fermenting has stopped, pour the liquid into a cask, bung tightly and leave for three months. Then put into another cask and leave it for ten months before bottling. Wait another year before drinking.

This is a simply-made wine but takes a long time to mature.

TONIC STOUT: Add 1 oz. dried stinging nettles, 1 oz. hops, and 8 oz. black (burnt) malt to 10 pt. water. Bring to the boil and then add $\frac{1}{4}$ oz. black liquorice and 2 unpeeled potatoes. The potatoes should be of medium size and perforated by a fork before being added to the mixture. Simmer gently until about 8 pt. liquid remains.

Strain into the earthenware dish and stir in 2 oz. brown sugar and 1 oz. of yeast. It is best to have mixed the sugar and yeast in a cupful of the cooled liquid beforehand. Leave covered for 24 hours, then bottle in the same way as described for horehound and wormwood beer.

WHEAT WINE: Place into a bowl 1 lb. wheat and 1 lb. finely-chopped potatoes (old ones will serve) with 2 lb. chopped sultanas, 4 lb. sugar, and the juice and rind of two grapefruits. Pour on to them 1 gal. hot water and stir until the sugar is dissolved.

When the water is lukewarm sprinkle 1 oz. of yeast into it and leave to ferment for three weeks.

Strain off into a gallon jar. Leave for six months, then bottle.

FURTHER NOTES: Never use anything except earthenware, glass, enamelled, and wooden utensils. On no account must fermenting take place in a metal container, or anything of metal be used in preparation.

Home-made wines can be produced quite freely provided they are not sold. This applies equally to private sale and to giving wine for subsequent re-sale, even for charity. Anyone wishing to make wine for sale must first seek advice from the customs and excise office.

Distilled spirits can never be made without a licence.

The majority of wines will clear easily. Vegetable wines take longer to clear than do flower wines. Some fruit wines may remain cloudy, but can be cleared by putting in the shells of 2 fresh eggs to 1 gal. liquid.

One of the reasons for making these wines is that it is a way of fixing the nutritive and medicinal properties of herbs and fruits so that they can be enjoyed when the fresh plant or fruit is not available. Properly made and properly taken they can give superior health and vitality.

What is called "blood heat" in wine making means when the temperature of the liquid is neither hot nor cold to the hand.

Refined sugar is unwholesome when taken ordinarily because it has a lack of natural properties other than sweetness. When used in wine making the balance is somewhat restored by fruits and natural plant sugar. Fortunately, most wines can be made by using other sweeteners such as honey, malt, and raisins. If honey is used it should be "clear" honey. If only cloudy honey is available it should be boiled with water first, and then skimmed to clarify it. This is not necessary with clear honey because the skimming after preparation of the wine will rid the mixture of impurities.

Today it is beyond the power of most of us to obtain really good water. Therefore tap water, filtered, chlorinated, denatured as it is, has to be used. Before our misguided reformers got busy, the best water was water from a fresh spring, with river water second best. Most rivers are now so polluted that it is no longer safe to use the water, and fewer people are able to find natural springs as so many have either been filled in, diverted, polluted, or built over. The principle still remains, that the better the water, the better the wine. If you can get good water, use it and value it.

Introducing yeast into your wine can be done in several ways, and it is a matter of preference. What is most important is the temperature of the liquid when the yeast is put in. The yeast works best at a temperature between 50 and 70 degrees Fahrenheit. If the liquid is too hot it will kill the yeast, and if too cold the yeast will remain inactive. But once it is working well it will produce its own heat to perpetuate unless the mixture is left in a cold place.

General Information

THIS general information on every main ingredient
mentioned in the treatments and the wines, is to
explain each item so that the reader may find out
something about the constituents of the remedies and
herbal wines.

Most of these ingredients can be obtained from the
greengrocer, the herbalist, or from the health food
stores.

The enthusiast can, if he wishes, collect the herbs
himself in the countryside, though great care should
be taken in doing so. Beware of the dangers of
crop-sprayed land. Children in particular should not
be allowed to eat plant leaves or other parts, unless
they have first been verified as being harmless. Fields,
woods, hedgerows, and other places which have been
chemically sprayed or treated should be avoided.

The ingredients have been listed alphabetically, and
the Latin names provided where appropriate.

AGRIMONY (*Agrimonia Eupatoria*): This herb
has pointed, dark green leaves. The flowers have
five yellow petals and grow off the main stem on long
spikes. Agrimony grows both in hedgerow and
meadow, to about 1 ft. in height, and blooms throughout the summer.

ALDER (*Glutinosa Alnus*): Do not confuse Alder with elder. The elder grows into a large tree, while the alder grows to only about 30 ft. in height as a tree. Usually found growing by streams or brooks, it bears rough, oval-shaped leaves, and two kinds of catkins in which are the male and female flowers.

ALLSPICE: A fragrant spice made from the berries of a tree which grows in Central America and the West Indies. So named because its smell is like that of a combination of cinnamon, cloves, and nutmeg.

ALMOND: The bitter variety of almond oil must be used carefully as it contains prussic acid, which is a poison. So do keep it away from children. Sweet almond oil is safe and has no ill effects, being the oil I have recommended for use in ear troubles. Almond flavouring used for cakes and custards is the bitter variety. Used with common sense it produces a delicious culinary result. A laurel leaf may be utilised in the same way, but it also contains prussic acid.

Almond trees grow in England, bearing white, pink, or red flowers. They bloom in the spring. The tree is ornamental and rarely grows to more than 10 ft. high.

ALOES: An evergreen plant, this is native to South Africa, although it thrives in greenhouses in Britain. It has thick, fleshy leaves and bears many tubular flowers. Bitter aloes, properly a drug, is obtained from the dried juice of the leaves. An oil is distilled from the wood of the aloes.

ALUM: Is a mineral substance, being the crystal-lized double sulphate of aluminium and potassium. It is obtained from many chemical sources including bauxite, ammonia, 'silver, sodium, as well as the original alunite. What are known as alum shales are to be found in England. Alum has several commercial uses, but in medicine it is a caustic and astringent.

AMMONIA: This is produced commercially as a by-product of coal gas.

APPLE (*Pyrus Malus*): The tree or bush bearing this popular fruit flourishes in Britain. Perhaps the most widely-eaten fruit in the western world, it is particularly suited to the health needs of Nordic peoples, and its value cannot be overstressed.

APPLE CIDER VINEGAR: No home should be without this sovereign cure-all. Taken twice a day, it will promote health more than anything else, with the possible exception of honey. If you find it too bitter to take on its own, then add honey in equal proportions and then add warm water.

APRICOT: A fruit tree of the order of Rosaceae, it was introduced into England from Asia in the seventeenth century.

ASPARAGUS (genus of *Liliaceae*): This plant grows wild in most parts of Europe. Medically useful for the substance it contains, called aspargine, which is valuable as a diuretic, and for its action on the urinary organs. Asparagus can be boiled as a soup, used as a sauce, or simply as a vegetable.

ASPHODEL (*Asphodelus Albus*): This is the white Asphodel which grows to a height of about three feet. It has a beautiful white flower, the flowers standing in spikes on top of the three divisions of the stalk. The flowers are streaked with purple on their tops with yellow threads in the middle.

The root is the part used in medicine.

AVENS (*Geum Urbanum*): Also known as wood avens and herb bennett. The plant is found abundantly in woods, copses, and shady hedgebanks.

The flowering stem reaches 3 ft. in height, bearing solitary bright yellow flowers from June to August.

BARBERRY (*Berberis Vulgaris*): A shrub having yellow flowers which give way to acid red berries. It grows in hedgerows to about 5 ft.

BARLEY (*Hordeum Sativum*): This is believed to be the first cereal ever cultivated by man. There are various sub-species used for different purposes such as malting, breadmaking, and distilling.

BEETROOT (*Chenopodiaceae*): Beetroot or beet is the name of two kinds of plant, one with a red, sweet root used as a vegetable, and the other with a white root, used for making sugar and commonly referred to as sugar beet.

BICARBONATE OF SODA: A salt in which two equivalents of carbonic acid combine with one equivalent of base. An antacid and stomachic.

BILBERRY (*Vaccinium Myrtillus*): A bush with many angular branches, and green-tinged rosy flowers which produce the dark blue edible berry. It is also known as whortleberry.

BINDWEED (*Convolvulus Arvensis*): The lesser bindweed is a weed found growing in fields and pastures. It has delicate pink or near-white flowers from June to September. Its leaves are spear-shaped and alternate.

BLACKBERRY (*Rubus Fruticosus*): Commonly known as the bramble. This well-known prickly herb produces a delicate and delicious fruit which is useful in cases of diarrhoea, because of its binding action upon the bowels. This is why pies are trationally eaten mixed with apple, to offset this action.

BLACKCURRANT (*Ribes Nigra*): The small, black, juicy fruit.

BLACKTHORN (*Prunus Spinosa*): This shrub, so commonly used for hedges, produces its white blossoms in March or April before the leaves appear. Its dark purple fruit is the sloe, which is a species of wild plum.

BLUESTONE: This is a sulphate of copper crystal having a caustic effect. For this reason, too strong a solution should not be used, especially for the eyes.

BORAX (*Biborate of Soda*): This useful gargle is a white, crystalline salt. It comes from the borax lakes in California, or from preparations of boracic acid from Tuscany.

BRAN: Is from the outer husk of corn when it is ground.

BRANDY: Old brandy containing the least alcohol is best as a medicine. The finest comes from Cognac, in Charente, France.

BREAD: Considering that bread is a dietary staple food for so much of the world, it is astonishing how careless people can be about it. Millions of unthinking people buy natureless white flour products, and disregard the healthful properties of wholemeal bread.

BROOM (*Cytisus Scoparius*): Grows to about 4 ft. in Britain and has dark green, spraying foliage. It bears bright yellow flowers which resemble those of the gorse bush. Like gorse, broom is found on heaths and moors.

BURDOCK (*Arctium Lappa*): Burdock has large leaves like those of rhubarb. Its flowers are small

74

and of a mauve-pinkish colour. When these turn to fruit they form burrs which cling to the clothing. It grows to a height of 4 or 5 ft.

CABBAGE (*Capum Brassica*): Common garden vegetable that it is, the medicinal properties of the cabbage are largely ignored. This is a pity, for as one old Romany said to me: "It holds the secret of long life".

CAMOMILE (*Anthemis Nobilis*): Camomile is sometimes spelt Chamomile. This is a strongly-scented herb which has yellow flowers or florets and a white ray. Some people seem to confuse camomile with calomel. But calomel is a drug, being a sub-chloride of mercury.

CAMPHOR (*Cinnamomum Camphora*): Grows in south-east Asia, notably Formosa, China, and Japan. What we know of as camphor is a hydrocarbon distilled from the wood of the tree. Another, slightly different camphor, known as Borneo or Sumatra camphor, is found in great crystallised blocks in the wood of a giant tree in the forests of those countries.

CARAWAY (*Carum Carui*): This biennial wild plant has leaves rather like those of the carrot. The seeds are really those tiny fruits so well known in cooking and confectionery.

CARROT (*Daucus Carota*): This root crop needs no elaboration to my readers, except to say that like cabbage its virtues should not be neglected.

CELERY (*Apium Graveolens*): Though considered as a popular table vegetable, celery is in reality a herb. Even among people with little or no knowledge of herbalism, celery is respected for its value in combating rheumatic disorders.

CHERRY: The cherry tree is of the rose order. There are several varieties, the best for eating purposes being the white-heart cherries. The cherry grows well in Kent, but its fruit is also imported from France and Belgium.

CHICKWEED (*Arenaria*): Sometimes called stitchwort. There are several varieties of this weed, all well known to the cage bird fancier as a food for his pets.

CINNAMON (*Cinnamomum*): Spice made from the bark of the Ceylon laurel.

CLOVES (*Eugenia Carophyllata*): Another aromatic spice, being the dried bud of an evergreen shrub growing in the East and West Indies.

COCONUT (*Cocos Nucifera*): The product of this economically important tree requires no elaboration.

COFFEE: It is well known that coffee is a stimulant, due to its alkaloid constituent called caffeine. This caffeine is similar in its effect to that of theine, which is the active principle of tea. Coffee quickens the mental faculties and removes drowsiness. If it is drunk to excess, however, it can cause indigestion, insomnia, and various nervous symptoms.

COLTSFOOT (*Tussilago Farfara*): Once called coughwort, this plant was used in ancient Greece for respiratory ailments. It shows bright yellow flowers in March, and can be found in or near woods. Sometimes it is mistaken for the dandelion.

COUCH GRASS (*Agropyrum Repens*): The stems of this grass will grow to four feet. It is regarded as a troublesome weed on arable land. Animals, especially cats, are aware of its health-giving properties, and will seek it out.

COWSLIP (*Primula Veris*): A herb belonging to the primrose order. It has stalked, drooping flowers with buff-yellow funnel-shaped corolla. These distinguish it from the yellow primrose.

CRANESBILL (*Geranium Dissectum*): Of the geranium family, its flowers are bluish-purple, with five petals. The seeds grow in a sharp pod resembling a bird's bill.

CRESOL: Is obtained from coal tar, being a light brown liquid much used as an antiseptic and disinfectant. It is a component of lysol.

CUCKOO PINT (*Arum Maculatum*): Sometimes called Wake Robin, this wild flower has arrow-shaped leaves, often marked with black or dull purple spots. When the leaves wither in autumn, their place is taken by a spike of scarlet berries. The leaves and berries are poisonous if eaten, but the leaf may be safely used in the treatment described for boils.

CUDWEED (*Gnaphalium Sylvaticum*): This is a dense, cottony herb with narrow leaves and small flower heads. The flower heads are enclosed by chaff-coloured scales which persist.

DANDELION (*Taraxacum Officinale*): This well-known wild flower has been used as a food as well as for medicinal purposes for centuries. Our own English word for it comes from the old French "dent-de-lion", or lion's tooth. This derives from the sharp points around the leaves. An excellent coffee is made from the root, which is suitable for those with heart troubles. Dandelion leaves are still eaten in salads in many parts of Europe as a matter of course.

DEMERARA SUGAR: Demerara is the name of the river which rises in the highlands of Guyana and enters the sea at Georgetown. It is also the name of a district between this river and the Berbice River. The soft brown sugar called Demerara was first produced there.

Sugar is a valuable food and a source of energy. There is a tendency, however, to take too much, and an excess is responsible for indigestion and obesity. A long period of over-eating, especially of carbohydrates, the sweet class of which are the sugars, can result in *diabetes mellitus*, or sugar diabetes.

White sugar should be avoided. The best sugars for health are unrefined, such as Demerara, and its by-product, molasses.

Honey is a natural invert sugar, and contains the best mixture of dextrose and laevulose. Dextrose sugar is also present in all fruits.

DOCK (*Rumex*): There are a dozen native species, including bitter, fiddle, yellow, water, and the sour dock or sorrel.

EAU-DE-COLOGNE: A spirituous preparation containing oils of rosemary, citron, orange, bergamot, neroli, and geranium. It has been produced since about 1700, and is very useful in the sick room for freshening purposes.

ELDER (*Sambucus Nigra*): A small tree or shrub seen growing in hedgerows. Its leaves are toothed and are five to a stem. Flowers appear in May and June and are creamy-white.

The purple-black berries, like the flowers, are used in home-made wines. Romanies have a great respect for the elder, and there is not any part of it that they do not use for some purpose or other.

ENDIVE (*Intypbum*): This herb is a kind of chicory, having curly pale leaves. It has similar properties to those of watercress.

EUCALYPTUS (*Eucalyptus Globulus*): A distillate of the fresh leaves of the Australian blue gum tree, the oil of the eucalyptus acts as an antiseptic, a disinfectant, and a deodorant.

EYEBRIGHT (*Euphrasia Officinalis*): This is a little annual herb found in meadows about 6 in. high. It blooms from May to September with small whitish flowers having a speck of yellow.

FENNEL (*Foeniculum Vulgare*): A fern-like perennial, this is a favourite of chefs for fish sauces and flavourings. Fennel is a beautiful plant with its golden flowers, and the Romans swore by it as an aid to digestion. It grows in unpromising rocky places, and also near the sea. Grazing animals are instinctively fond of it, and it has many veterinary uses.

FIG (*Ficus Carica*): Dried figs are always good to eat and, like other fruits, are better for children than sweets. Some people cannot cope with the hard skins of figs, however, and some find that they cause them indigestion. The skins can be discarded if necessary, or the figs may be softened by boiling them in milk.

FISH: This word as loosely applied to all sea creatures is what is meant here by fish. Any fresh sea food is good for you, and the value of it has been known to man for almost as long as man has existed. Fish food is particularly good for the Nordic type of human being. Edible freshwater fish are good too, although not as good for you as those from the sea.

FLUELLIN (*Veronica Officinalis*): There are two varieties of this weed that grows at the edges of cornfields. They both have long creepers lying along the ground. They have hairy leaves and small flowers. One variety bears a yellow and purple flower, while the other bears a white flower. Both have small black seeds. Fluellin is sometimes called speedwell.

FORMALIN: This deodorant and disinfectant is a 40 per cent solution of formaldehyde in water. Formaldehyde is a gas produced by passing vapour of methyl alcohol over red hot copper. I have known people to use formalin as a food preservative, but this is not to be recommended, as it is noxious when used for this purpose. Be careful not to overdo the quantity when using it for any reason.

FROGBIT (*Hydrocharis Morsus Ranae*): This small, floating aquatic herb has kidney-shaped leaves, their undersides of a reddish colour. The bulbs sink to the bottom of ponds in the autumn, then rise to the surface again in spring to throw out leaves. It has white flowers.

GINGER (*Zingibar Officinale*): Rootstock of a perennial reed-like herb, ginger has been known as a spice from antiquity. Grown throughout the tropics, the best varieties come from Jamaica and from China.

GLYCERINE (*Trihydric Alcohol*): This thick, colourless liquid is much used in pharmaceutical preparations. Glycerine is obtained from fats.

GRAPEFRUIT (*Citrus Decumana*): This fruit of an Asian evergreen tree was once called a shaddock. It is now much cultivated in California as its slightly acid taste has proved to make a pleasant beginning to a meal.

GREATER CELANDINE (*Chelidonium Majus*): Growing to 2, and even 3 ft. in height, this herb of the poppy order can be found near houses, on the side of the road, or on waste ground. It has bright yellow flowers with four petals to each one. The leaves are long, being green on top and grey underneath. The yellow juice is almost as good as that of the dandelion for the treatment of warts.

GROUNDSEL (*Senecio Vulgaris*): Groundsel is a common herbaceous plant to be found everywhere in Britain. Its small yellow flowers are succeeded by white, fluffy seed heads. The leaves are alternate and deeply cut, with irregularly toothed lobes.

GROUND IVY (*Nepeta Hederacea*): This trailing flower is very abundant in the grass at the bottom of hedgerows. It is one of the earliest flowers to appear in spring. The purple-blue flowers are in sets of three to six. Ground ivy has no relationship to the real ivy. It is also called ale hoof because it was once used in brewing for its tonic qualities.

HAWKWEED: See Mousear.

HONEY: There was a time in Britain when sugar was an imported luxury available only to the wealthy. In those days honey was generally used as a sweetener. Such are our topsy-turvy economics and advertising pressures, that today sugar is a commonplace and honey is bought mainly by the health-conscious. Fortunately there are several varieties on sale, from orange flower honey to honey collected from un-sprayed jungle trees, and one can select a personal choice. Do not buy blended honey as this is often mixed with sugar. The constituents of pure honey are given under Demerara sugar.

HOPS (*Humulus Lupulus*): Female catkins of the hop plant, hops are chiefly used for flavouring beer. The plant is a perennial climbing herb with twining stems, bearing flowers in green, scaly cones. After flowering the hops develop small yellow glands secreting the special principle of the herb.

HOREHOUND (black) (*Ballota Nigra*): The black horehound is also known as madweed, and sometimes as gypsy wort. It grows to 1 to 2 ft. high and has downy and wrinkled leaves. Its flowers are purple.

HOREHOUND (white) (*Marrubium Vulgare*): Sometimes called madweed, like the black horehound. Its branches are covered with white down. The leaves are on stalks, and are very wrinkled. Flowering in summer and autumn, the white horehound has small, greyish-white flowers in dense clusters.

HORSE CHESTNUT (*Aesculus Hippocastanum*): Schoolboys know this tree well as the one which provides them with "conkers", the word being a corruption of conquerors. Introduced into England for ornamental purposes in the 1600's, the horse chestnut is indeed beautiful with its dense and spreading foliage, symmetrically proportionate to its height of about a hundred feet. The flowers are pink and white, and beloved by pollinating bees.

HORSERADISH (*Cochlearia Armoracia*): The pungent root of this herb provides the well-known condiment, and the oil extracted from horseradish is an antidote to scurvy. The root of the herb is very powerful and will spread and push through almost any obstacle, so horseradish is not popular in the garden.

HOUSELEEK (*Sempervivum Tectorum*): A familiar succulent herb in the countryside, houseleek grows on cottage roofs and walls in rosettes of fleshy leaves with pink flowers. It has no affinity with the leek proper.

HYSSOP (*Hyssopus Officinalis*): This small aromatic plant is a native of the Mediterranean shores. It has blue flowers and lance-like leaves.

ISINGLASS: This whitish, gelatinous substance is obtained from the air bladders of certain kinds of fish, notably the sturgeon. It is used for clarifying liquor, and in cookery.

IVY (*Hedera Helix*): This common evergreen climber can be found on walls and trees. The yellow-green flowers appear in September and October and are succeeded by small yellow or black berries.

JALAP (*Ipomaea*): Imported from Jalapa in Mexico, this purgative drug is obtained from the resin of the tuberous roots of the plant. Jalap is well known to the medical profession in the treatment for dropsy.

LADIES SLIPPER (*Lotus Corniculatu*): A pasture and downs flower, ladies slipper is also known as bird's foot trefoil. It has trailing branches and its flowers are in spreading heads of from three to ten, bright yellow in colour, tinted with red. From June to October the fields are made bright with the ladies slipper.

LARD (*Adeps Praeparatus*): The fat or lard of pigs is used as the basis for ointments, but to prevent it from becoming rancid 3 per cent of benzoin is usually added, when the lard becomes, in medical parlance, *Adeps Benzoatus*.

LEEK (*Allium Porrum*): A well-known hardy biennial, this bulbous herb is the national emblem of Wales.

LEMON (*Citrus Medica*): Large quantities of lemons are imported into Britain from the Mediterranean and South Africa. The rind is used for candied peel and the juice is well known in cookery and in medicine.

The virtues of lemon juice as a slimming agent are familiar to women. The juice is best taken first thing, in hot water and without sugar. Lemon juice run on the hands will keep them soft. Two halves of lemon peel boiled with the clothes make an excellent bleach and also keeps clothing free of soap scum. Discoloured elbows will revert to a normal colour if the elbows are placed in halves of lemon peel for a while.

Another use for lemon peel is to remove the smell of grease from a pan. Rub the pan with the inside of half the peel, and it will soon be clean and fresh.

LIME (*Tilia Europaea*): The lime tree or linden has clustered yellowish-white flowers and heart-shaped leaves. It was introduced into England in Tudor days. The wood is white and fairly soft.

LIMEWATER: Oxide of calcium broken down into slaked lime, or calcium hydroxide is soluble in water, forming the solution known as limewater.

LINSEED (*Linum Usitatissimum*): Linseed oil is made from ripened and dried flax seeds.

LIQUORICE (*Glycyrrhiza*): Liquorice comes from the long, woody roots of a perennial Mediterranean herb. English liquorice growing is declining owing to difficulty of finding labour to dig the root. Most of it is imported from Italy and Spain.

MACE: This spice is prepared from the fleshy outer covering of the nutmeg.

MALE FERN (*Dryopteris Filixmas*): Flowerless plants or perennial herbs of which there are some fifty varieties in Britain.

MALT: Is a name given to partially germinated grain of various cereals, but it is chiefly barley that is meant.

MANDRAKE (*Mandragora*): This genus of perennial herbs of the potato order has long been associated with magic and witchcraft. It is a stemless plant with thick, fleshy roots. The forked growth of these roots simulates the lower limbs of a human being. The mandrake is mentioned in the Bible in Genesis XXX. It grows mainly around the Mediterranean.

MARJORAM (*Origanum Vulgare*): Wild marjoram grows at the edges of woods, to about a height of 2 ft. It has purple flowers and oval-shaped toothed leaves.

MARMALADE: This preserve was originally made from quinces, but it is now usually made from Seville oranges. The best marmalade for health, however, is one made from apricots.

MEADOW-SWEET (*Spiraea Ulmaria*): This flower is also known as bridewort and queen of the meadows. It is found in wet meadows and on the banks of streams and rivers, flowering from June to August. The flowers are small and yellowish-white in colour, and though they do not produce nectar they attract insects by their sweet smell. Meadow-sweet is a useful ingredient in herb beers.

MERCURY (*Hydrargyrum*): Sometimes called quicksilver, this metallic element is extensively used in medicine. It is extracted from the sulphide cinnabar. Too frequent application of mercurial ointments can cause dermatitis, as these antiseptic solutions are extremely poisonous.

MILK: The young of all mammals depend on milk

for their entire subsistence at the earliest period of life. Milk contains, therefore, all the ingredients of a diet. These include proteins, fats, carbohydrates, salts, vitamins, and water. It should be remembered, however, that the milk of different animals varies in the proportions of these substances, so that the milk of one animal does not necessarily suit another. The milk from cows is usually best for most adult humans, but it has to be modified for infants.

MINT (*Mentha Spicata*): There are numerous varieties of this herb, but the spicata is the one usually found in gardens. All the fourteen varieties native to Britain have a similar characteristic flavour. Since the time of ancient Greece, mint has been known as a blood tonic.

MOUSEAR (*Hieracium Pilosella*): Also known as hawkweed, this common weed is found on lawns, its runners spreading out with the leaves in little rosettes close to the ground. The flowers are of a lemon colour.

MUGWORT: See Wormwood.

MUTTON FAT: Animal fat consists of a mixture of three fats, olein, palmitin, and stearin. The proportionate constituents in mutton fat make it useful in winter for chapped hands. Keep it away from your lips as it can cause unwanted hair to grow on the lower part of the face.

NASTURTIUM (*Nasturtium Officinale*): This is the perennial aquatic herb popularly called watercress. It is found all over Britain wherever there is fresh water. The main stem may be nearly 1 in. thick and up to 2 ft. long. Floating on the water, this stem roots from its lower side. From May to October the Nasturtium bears small white flowers. The long narrow leaves are heart-shaped, growing in pairs, with one larger odd leaf at the end of each branch or midrib.

The name nasturtium is also given to a South American flower of the geranium order.

NETTLE (*Urtica Dioica*): This is the stinging nettle, dark green and growing to 4 ft. The male and female flowers, green in colour, are carried on the same plant and in clusters. Much of the chlorophyll on the market in various products is from the nettle, which is a rich source. Nettles should not be neglected as a vegetable, for when boiled they are as good as spinach in every way.

NUTMEG (*Myristica Fragrans*): The well-known nutmeg is the seed-kernel from the fleshy fruit of a bushy evergreen tree which grows in Malaya, Indonesia, and the West Indies. Although a popular spice, too much nutmeg should not be taken at once, as a large dose acts as a poison. Normally used, the nutmeg is harmless.

OATS (*Avena Sativa*): Like barley, this is another cereal grass cultivated in ancient times. Kiln-dried, they become the basis for porridge and other breakfast cereals such as rolled oats and oat flakes.

OAK (*Quercus Robur*): One of the most common trees in the countryside, the oak sometimes grows to nearly 120 ft. high. Oak trees are noted for living to a great age, a thousand years being not unusual. Its leaves are rounded and irregular. The groups of acorns are on stalks on the common oak, but not on the Durmast oak, which is a similar species found growing on lighter soil.

OLIVE (*Olea Europaea*): This small evergreen tree flourishes in the Mediterranean area, and also grows in Australia, South Africa and in California. The oil extracted from the ripe berries is much used in Middle Eastern diets, often replacing butter and animal fats. It is also much used for medical purposes in all parts of the world.

ONION (*Allium Cepa*): This well-known vegetable is a herb of the lily order.

ORANGE (*Citrus Aurantium*): Another evergreen, the orange tree has spread in cultivation to many countries since its origins in the Indo-Chinese peninsula. The Arabs introduced it into Asia Minor, and later took it to Spain. All the varieties of the fruit are valuable for their content of mineral salts and vitamins A, B, and especially C.

PARSLEY PIERT (*Alchemilla Arvensis*): Once known as parsley breakstone because of it being used to dissolve stones in the kidneys, this herb grows to some 6 in. It has large leaves with toothed lobes and small green flowers.

PARSNIP (*Peucedanum Sativum*): The parsnip has been cultivated since Roman times. It is palatable and nutritious, and contains sugar. Its long white tapering root is an excellent food.

PEACH (*Prunus Persica*): Fruit tree of the rose order. Most market supplies of the fruit are grown in France, Delaware and California.

PEPPERCORN: This is the dried, round berry of black pepper. The usual table condiment called pepper is simply the berries ground into powder. Black pepper is made from the whole berry; white pepper is produced by removing the skin of the berry first, by soaking the berry in water and then rubbing it off.

PEPPERMINT (*Mentha Piperita*): A perennial European herb, this can be found growing wild in

Britain. Related to mint, as previously described, the pepper variety is used in medicine as an antispasmodic. Peppermint has the characteristic creeping rootstock of the other mints, and coarse-toothed leaves.

PILEWORT (*Ranunculus Ficaria*): A herb of the buttercup family, pilewort is also known as the lesser celandine. It is found all over Britain. The brilliant yellow star-like flowers appear in spring and bloom to the middle of May.

PIMPERNEL (*Anagallis Arvensis*): Known also as the scarlet pimpernel this flower is common in gardens, fields, and on waste ground. The scarlet flowers appear singly on very long slender stalks from the axils of the leaves, during the months from May to November. The leaves are stalkless and oval in shape.

The petals close every day at about 2 p.m. If they are closed before that time it is a certain sign that rain is on the way.

PINE (*Pinus Sylvestris*): There are two main species of this evergreen tree which are well known in Britain. The *pinus sylvestris* or Scots pine averages 100 ft. in height. Pines differ from firs in having the needle-shaped leaves clustered in twos and fives.

The other well-known variety of pine is the stone pine, in Latin, *Pinus Pinea*. It has a more squat appearance due to its wider spread of branches, which sometimes exceeds its height.

PLANTAIN (*Plantago Major*): A common herb having very broad leaves on short stalks. The flowers are on tall spikes and are purple in colour. It is also called ripple grass, way bread, and lamb's tongue:

PORRIDGE: Oatmeal porridge is the best kind for health. Oats were known to have been cultivated in the Bronze Age.

POTATO (*Solanum Tuberosum*): It may surprise readers to know that this well-known food is a tuber of a herb of the nightshade order. It was grown by the ancient Incas, and reached sixteenth-century Spain from Peru.

POULTRY: Used in this book as the collective name for all domestic fowls such as ducks, geese, turkeys, and chickens.

PRIMROSE (*Primula Vulgaris*): Abundant in open woods and in hedgerows. The primrose flowers during April and May. Its flowers are on long, slender stalks of a pinkish colour.

PRUNE (*Prunus Domestica*); This dried plum has highly nutritive qualities. Perhaps the best prunes are those from plums grown in the Loire valley, sometimes called French plums.

PUMPKIN (*Cucurbita Pepo*): This herb of the gourd order was first introduced into England in Tudor days.

QUASSIA (*Quassia Amara*): A bitter wood, quassia is regularly used in medicine. Originally from Surinam, but there is now a West Indian substitute bitter wood, *Picraena Excelsa*, generally known as Jamaica Quassia.

The infused chips, as well as having tonic properties can also be used in place of hops when brewing beer.

RADISH (*Raphanus Sativus*): A common garden herb which can be eaten raw or cooked. Some people find them difficult to digest when raw, and boiling slowly for an hour or so in salted water will make them palatable.

RAGWORT (*Senecio Jacobea*): Found in neglected places and by roadsides, ragwort is a tough, ubiquitous herb. With an erect branching leafy stem, its name is justified by its broken-up leaves in toothed lobes. The bright yellow flowers, about an inch across, appear from June to October, although in the far south they may even be seen at Christmas time. The stem grows from 1 to 4 ft.

RAISIN (*Vitis Vinifera*): The raisin is the dried ripe fruit of certain white varieties of grape. There are sub-varieties of raisins such as the Malaga, muscatel, pudding, Elemes, and seedless sultanas. They all contain the same nutritional value, however, and vary only in taste according to where they were grown and how they were dried.

RASPBERRY (*Rubus Idaeus*): This perennial can be found in woods and on heaths, flowering from June till August.

RED MERCURIC OXIDE: All oxides are compounds formed by the combination of an element with oxygen. Many of the metallic elements form oxides.

RHUBARB (*Rheum*): Although the stalks of this herbaceous plant are edible, the leaves are poisonous to many people, and are best left severely alone. The rhizome, or root, contains a substance resembling cathartic acid. This gives it the value of a purgative which is followed by a binding action.

ROSEMARY (*Rosmarinus Officinalis*): This hardy evergreen perennial shrub grows between 2 and 3 ft. in height. Oil of rosemary is extracted from its fragrant green leaves. The small, violet flowers appear in early summer. Used sparingly, the finely-chopped leaves add a delicious flavour to salads, soup, and stew.

RUE (*Ruta Graveolens*): Also known as the herb of grace, and the poor man's heal-all. Grows best in soil containing lime. It is a small shrub of south European origin. The leaves are serrated and of a dull, bluish-green. The flowers are of a greenish-yellow colour. Rue is very hardy and was popular in Elizabethan gardens. It will grow to 2 ft. in height.

RUM: This spirit is distilled from cane sugar molasses fermented by yeast. Some inferior grades are made from cane juice and sometimes from beet molasses. Jamaica, Demerara, and Martinique are the chief places for the manufacture of rum.

SAFFRON (*Crocus Sativu*): A perennial herb growing in both Europe and Asia. The leaves are rather like grass, and it bears purple flowers. One of the many herbs used in cooking as well as in medicine.

SAGE (*Salvia Officinalis*): Well known as a stuffing to accompany rich or greasy dishes, sage is an excellent aid to digestion. It will grow in almost any soil, but likes plenty of sun. For drying, sage should be gathered at the end of June. It bears purple flowers and has oblong leaves.

SALT (*Sodium Chloride*): This mineral deposit occurs throughout nature, in the sea, in rock form, and in brine springs. The rock salt of Britain is found in the Triassic beds of Cheshire and the neighbouring counties. Although salt is essential to diet, many people take far too much of it as a seasoning.

It should be possible to get sufficient intake from vegetable sources, without having recourse to the salt cellar.

SALTPETRE (*Potassium Nitrate*): An elemental metal belonging to the alkaline group, saltpetre is a normal constituent of the body. Too much, however, like sodium, is depressing to the heart and the nervous system.

SARSAPARILLA (*Smilax Officinalis*): Sarsaparilla contains a bitter principle known as parillin, and some starch. It comes from Central America.

SELF-HEAL (*Prunella Vulgaris*): Found abundantly in damp pastures, this herb is a perennial with a creeping root and flowering branches. The stem is square and the stalked leaves are long, oval-shaped, and with toothed margins. The flowers are mostly purple, but sometimes crimson or white. Its flowering period is July to September.

SENNA (*Cahassia Acutifolia*): A tropical herb, senna is well-known as a laxative. The pods are used for a mild purgative, and the dried leaves for a stronger one.

SHERRY: Several Spanish white wines are called sherry, the pale, dry varieties being the Manzanilla sherries, and the sweet kinds being Olorosa. Other varieties are the Vino Fino, Montilla, and Amontillado. The best comes from Jerez or Xeres, in the region of Cadiz.

SPINACH (*Spinacia*): An edible herb which is still a popular table vegetable. The great virtue of spinach is the fact that it is easily digested and its action is gentle upon the system. Quite harmless too as a colouring agent in such things as jellies, and this is something which cannot be said of all colouring matter.

STRAWBERRY (*Fragaria Vesca*): A native of Britain, rightly valued for its delicious fruit.

SULPHUR: The old name for sulphur is brimstone, and it is found as incrustations in volcanic rock, or in crystal form in clay. A non-metallic element, its uses in medicine are internally as a laxative, and externally for numerous skin diseases. Care must be taken when using sulphur, as the drug is an irritant to the skin. Sulphur candles can be used for fumigation of infected rooms.

SULTANAS: See Raisin.

SWEET CHESTNUT (*Castanea Sativa*): Sometimes called the Spanish chestnut. Like so many other things, it is believed to have been introduced into Britain by the Romans. The tree averages 100 ft. in height and is identifiable by the spiralling upward effect of the bark. An attractive aspect of this tree is the edible nut it produces.

TALLOW (*Excaecaria Sebifera*): A Chinese tree, the seeds of which are covered with a grease from which candles can be made. There is another tallow tree grown in Africa, *Pentadesma Butyracea*, producing a similar grease.

Most tallow used in Europe, however, is that obtained from the broken-down fat of such animals as sheep.

TEA (*Thea Sinensis*): Of the Camellia genus of plants, tea has been known for many centuries in China, but only came to England about the year 1645. Since Britain is the largest consumer of tea in the world, the merits of the beverage need not be enlarged upon here.

Too much tea, especially strong or over-infused tea, can result in nervous disorders, insomnia, dyspepsia, and constipation.

THYME (*Thymus Serpyllum*): Wild thyme is a delightfully fragrant herb. Its flowers are of a rosy-purple colour, and the leaves are small and stalked. The plant is usually found on high pasture land from June to September.

TOMATO (*Lycopersicum Esculentum*): The fruit of the tomato plant is very rich in vitamins A, B, and C. Tomatoes also contain a most useful amount of sulphur. People who suffer from gout should not eat tomatoes.

TREACLE: Is made from molasses, which substance is a by-product of sugar refining. It has considerable food value.

TURNIP (*Brassica Campestus*): The white turnip is grown for the table, and both leaves and roots can be used. The golden turnip, or swede, is grown as cattle food, especially for winter feeding. It is also eaten by humans, being quite suitable, and also keeping longer than the white variety.

TURPENTINE: Oil of turpentine is distilled from a resin obtained from various pine trees. It helps to relieve pains in muscles and joints, and is useful rubbed on the chest for bronchitic discomfort.

VASELINE: This is the proprietary name for a brand of soft paraffin. It forms the basis of many ointments.

VINEGAR (*Acetic acid*): In Britain this is usually made from malted barley.

WATERCRESS: See Nasturtium.

WHEAT (*Triticum Sativum*): This is
to be the most important cereal food of tem
climates, and after rice is the most widely-used gra

WHITE BEETROOT: That variety of beet usually
called sugar beet.

WILLOW: The name given to any tree or shrub
of the genus Salix, many species being found in the
northern hemisphere. The tree is known for its strong,
pliant branches. The leaves are long, and the flowers
are borne on catkins which appear before the leaves.

WOOD SAGE (*Teucrium Scorodonia*): Before
flowering, this might be mistaken for the ordinary
sage. But wood sage bears yellow flowers in sprays.
It can be found in woods from July to September.

WORMWOOD (*Artemisia Absinthium*): A herb
bearing many drooping dingy yellow flowers during
August and September. It grows to about 3 ft. in
height. This plant has a long history, being regarded
by the ancient Greeks as sacred to Artemis, or
Diana. It is well known in Japanese herbal lore, and
was used by the Aztecs in religious rites.

Another species, mugwort (*Artemisia Vulgaris*) is
found on roadsides and waste spaces, being a perennial,
aromatic herb. It has a red, rough stem from 2 to 4 ft.
high. The flower heads are small and gathered into
short woolly spikes, containing reddish-yellow flowers.
Mugwort flowers from June to September.

YEAST: This is the minute fungi of the saccharo-
myces. With sugar, yeast forms an enzyme called
zymase which promotes fermentation.